ACCIDENTS IN NORTH AMERICAN MOUNTAINEERING

VOLUME 9 • NUMBER 2 • ISSUE 60

2007

THE AMERICAN ALPINE CLUB
GOLDEN

THE ALPINE CLUB OF CANADA
BANFF

ISSN: 0065-082X
ISBN13: 978-1-933056-06-7

Manufactured in the United States

Published by
The American Alpine Club, Inc.
710 Tenth Street, Suite 100
Golden, CO 80401

Cover Illustrations
Front: A search team from Eugene Mountain Rescue ascending the Cooper Spur on Mount Hood in December of 2006. Photograph by Steve Cash. (N.B.: See pages 55–59.)

Back: John Sauerteig following on the Grande Gendarme of Bugaboo Spire in 1957. He was being belayed by Ted Church. Robert Jones led the pitch without placing any pitons—because they had left them in basecamp. Notice the then state-of-the-art equipment, including the "soft" helmet. Photograph by Robert W. Jones.

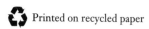 Printed on recycled paper

CONTENTS

SAFETY COMMITTEES 2006

The American Alpine Club
Aram Attarian, John Dill, Mike Gauthier, Renny Jackson,
Daryl Miller, Jeff Sheetz, and John E. (Jed) Williamson (Chair)

The Alpine Club of Canada
Peter Amann (Jasper), Rob Chisnall (Kingston), Dave McCormick
(Chair), Scott McLarty (Calgary), Frank Pianka (Thunder Bay)
Selina Swets (Vancouver)

ACCIDENTS IN
NORTH AMERICAN MOUNTAINEERING
Fifty-Ninth Annual Report of the Safety Committees
of The American Alpine Club and The Alpine Club of Canada

This is the sixtieth issue of *Accidents in North American Mountaineering*. At the time of publication, narratives and data from Canada were not available.

United States: Once again there were too many reports of rappel errors (ten) and lowering errors (five). The tragedy of the year was the loss of Todd Skinner, who fell to his death after his harness loop parted while he was rappelling in Yosemite Valley. It is hard to understand how such an experienced climber could find himself in this situation.

The reader will find a lengthy analysis of the Sue Nott/Karen McNeill disappearance from their route on the Infinite Spur on Mount Foraker. It illustrates the level of care and thoroughness that our park rangers who are involved in rescue operations will go to try to find causes and alert future climbers.

We try not to lay blame and name-call in this annual report. That is why we appreciate it when climbers submit their personal accounts of mishaps and include such comments as, "I simply wasn't being careful enough," and, "That was dumb!" in their analyses. There are a few good self-reports in this edition.

Another disturbing kind of accident that seems to be making an annual appearance is the tumbling fall that is the result of glissading with crampons attached (seven). One case in particular was what appeared to be a deliberate glissade—rather than a down-climb—on a very icy surface. The predictable result was several fractured bones. Four of the seven incidents reported happened on Mount Washington (NH)—three in Tuckerman Ravine, and one in Huntington Ravine.

While we are still not getting reports from some key areas, there are some web-based resources that often provide good information and accident stories. One of the primary ones is www.supertopo.com. A good one for Mount Washington is www.tuckerman.org. As always, we seek help from the climbing corners of the country.

Mount Hood made headlines again, including a lot of media coverage. I was the chief investigator of the tragic 1986 Oregon Episcopal School accident in which seven students and two teachers perished during a storm because they failed to turn back. State legislators raised the issue then as to whether locator beacons should be required for every climber. (Cellphones weren't in as yet.) This year, in the aftermath of the stranded climbers who

1

were not found in time, legislators again introduced a bill mandating that climbers going above 10,000 feet carry locator devices and GPS receivers with cellphones. In an op-ed piece, Jim Whitaker brought forward the key issues:

"The accidents on Mount Hood remind us that nobody can move in a severe mountain storm, not even a rescuer. Sending a distress call could result in rescuers being sent out into a life-threatening situation for no good reason, which is why most rescue workers oppose the law. And waiting for rescuers summoned by beacons can be more deadly than moving on…

"Most important, though, we need to meet the wilderness on its own terms. Laws and locators cannot replace careful attention, knowledge, and personal responsibility."

From October 24–26, the Wilderness Risk Management Conference will be held at The Banff Centre. (Go to www.NOLS.edu/wrmc/ for information on the program and registration.)

In addition to the dedicated individuals on the Safety Committee, we are grateful to the following—with apologies for any omissions—for collecting data and for helping with the report: Hank Alacandri, Dave Brown, Chris Harder, Tom Moyer, Erik Nelson, Leo Paik, Justin Preisendorfer, Robert Speik, Eric White, all individuals who sent in personal stories, and, of course, George Sainsbury.

John E. (Jed) Williamson
Managing Editor
7 River Ridge Road
Hanover, NH 03755
e-mail: jedwmsn@sover.net

Edwina Podemski
Canadian Editor
700 Phipps McKinnon Building
10020-101A Avenue
Edmonton, Alberta T5J 3G2
e-mail: cwep@compusmart.ab.ca

MEXICO

FALL ON ROCK, FREE-SOLO CLIMBING
El Potrero Chico, The Scariest Ride in the Park
On November 24, Jimmy Rae Forester (43) fell to his death while free-solo-ing The Scariest Ride in the Park (5.9). He had failed to return to camp and was found the next day at the base of this 40-pitch climb.

(Editor's Note: The following excerpts are from an article in the March 2007 is-sue of Rock and Ice. *"Forester was well known throughout Oklahoma and Texas, where he repeated the runout trad routes and established a slew of his own, always in the ground-up, onsight style he loved. Imbued with a deep sense of climbing history, Forester sought to preserve traditional ways.*

"Forester was dedicated to protecting climbing resources and was an environmental activist.")

UNITED STATES

ISCHEMIA AND CORONARY OCCLUSION
Alaska, Mount McKinley, West Rib/Cassin

On April 26, H. Dean Barkley, Jr. (47) and his partner were attempting to climb the West Rib and Cassin routes of Denali. Barkley had a history of cardiac problems. Approximately two hours out of basecamp, he experienced a cardiac event. The team was able to return to the Kahiltna Basecamp without assistance. They arrived at 2100 and contacted the NPS Ranger stationed there. At 2115 Ranger Gordy Kito contacted Talkeetna via radio, advised the IC that they had a probable cardiac event occurring and requested immediate evacuation of the patient. The Lama was scrambled from Talkeetna at 2153 to perform the evacuation, arrived at the 7,200-foot camp at 2229 and returned at 2300. The patient was placed into an ambulance and then transferred to Life Flight at 2320. He was ultimately diagnosed and treated for severe ischemia and a coronary occlusion.

Analysis

Injuries and illnesses are to be expected during a mountaineering expedition and, unfortunately, can occur regardless of planning. However, in this case the climber had suffered a coronary blockage six months prior and had had a stint inserted. The patient was taking several potent coronary drugs for his condition but was also forthcoming about his condition when questioned about any existing medical problems or history during the mandatory climbing briefing conducted before they flew onto the mountain. Prior to the climb, he had consulted with his physician and had passed a stress test.

It was fortunate that this happened at the start of his planned climb. Had it occurred later while on the technical part of the route, the evacuation would have been much more difficult and the outcome could have been different.

Climbing Denali requires a monumental physical effort, and any attempt to climb it, especially via one of the more challenging routes, requires individuals to be at peak physical capacity. (Source: From a report by John A. Loomis, Ranger)

FALL INTO CREVASSE—UNABLE TO BE RESCUED QUICKLY BECAUSE OF POSITION
Alaska, Wrangell Mountains, Mount Bona

On May 17, Will Hurst (56), who was climbing with two guides and another client, fell through a snow bridge. At the time, they were on snowshoes and at an elevation of 9,700 feet. He was roped and leading when the bridge collapsed and he dropped 20 feet, becoming wedged in a such a way that he could not breathe. He suffocated quickly. (Source: From a report by Kyle Hopkins in *The Anchorage Daily News* on May 19, 2006)

(Editor's Note: At 16,550 feet, Mount Bona is the fourth highest peak in the U.S. Marshall Neeck, Chief Ranger for the Wrangell St. Elias National Park and Reserve, told the reporter that there have been one or two fatalities a year in the park in recent years.)

FALL ON SNOW—SKI MOUNTAINEERING, UNABLE TO SELF-ARREST
Alaska, Mount McKinley, Orient Express

The "Whiskey Expedition" departed the 14,200-foot camp at noon on May 25 for a summit bid via the upper West Rib of Denali. Their plan was to summit and then accomplish a ski descent via the Orient Express. Two days prior to this they had skied on the lower portion of the Orient (up to 16,000 feet) and had judged the snow conditions to be excellent. The day preceding their climb they approached the medical camp Ranger John Loomis and inquired about the conditions on the upper Orient. A guided expedition had just descended that area and had described the conditions as being very hard snow interspersed with blue ice, not what one would really consider good or safe skiing conditions. Furthermore, blue ice could be seen upon the upper reaches. This information was conveyed to Edward Maginn (33), who stated that they hadn't found those conditions lower down and that they would continue with their plan. The group climbed up through the Orient Express and reached the summit at 2200. They commenced their ski descent, reaching the entry couloir to the Orient at 2300. Maginn was the first one down the route, and after descending the first 1,000 feet without incident, reported losing his balance after skiing over sastrugi. Maginn later stated that he had recollections of tumbling down the slope, but did not remember arriving at the 15,700-foot level. His two partners witnessed the fall and watched until he disappeared from view. They then called the 14,200-foot camp via FRS radio and advised the rangers there of the accident. The rangers went outside and could immediately identify the location of the fallen climber. While patrol members were being alerted, a spotting scope was used to get a closer view of the incident site. Through the spotting scope it was observed that the climber was just below the bergschrund and was not moving. A plan was formulated to dispatch two teams: one a hasty team to evaluate the climber and the second to follow with technical rescue gear and a cascade litter. In addition, two climbing guides, Freddie Wilkinson and Adam Knoff, were made emergency hires to assist with the rescue. Five to seven minutes later, prior to the hasty team's departure, the climber was observed to exhibit movement, followed by removing his pack and then initiating a descent by sliding on his butt and then finally a staggering walk. While on that descent, he appeared to punch into a hidden crevasse up to his waist.

The hasty team expedited their departure and exited the camp at 2316. At 2328 contact was made with Maginn—who was still walking unsteadily. His face was bloody and he appeared to be very dazed. He had to be told to stop. He did not appear to be aware of the rescue team's presence. C-spine control was established and an immediate medical exam accomplished. The second team arrived ten minutes later, and based on the mechanism of injury, Maginn was placed on a long spine board and sledded to the medical camp for further medical treatment. Both teams and the patient arrived at the medical camp at 2347, and his two partners arrived at 2355 and 0014 respectively. They had stopped where Maginn had landed and retrieved his pack and one ski pole. Medical control was notified and a plan formulated to evacuate the patient the following morning with the SA-315B Lama. This evacuation occurred at 1047 on the 26th. Maginn was flown to Alaska Regional Hospital, where he was diagnosed with only a fractured nose and corneal abrasions.

Analysis

Mr. Maginn was extremely fortunate to have survived this fall, let alone survived it with minimal injuries. It could be argued that the three climbers did not exercise good judgment in skiing down the face, especially after being informed of the current conditions; however, they did climb the same route that they eventually attempted to ski down and were able to conduct an on-site analysis on which to base their decision. The three purportedly had extensive backcountry ski experience and had conducted an intelligent climb and acclimatization schedule prior to the accident.

These three climbers skied the lower half of their route and climbed the upper half and did not attempt it "blind." That the accident occurred is unfortunate, but the overwhelming reason this climber did not perish is because he and his partners took it upon themselves to wear helmets. Maginn's helmet was significantly damaged. It is likely he would have perished had he not been wearing it. (Source: John Loomis, Ranger)

FROSTBITE—INADEQUATE CLOTHING (NO OVERBOOTS) AND INADEQUATE CARE OF EXTREMITIES
Alaska, Mount McKinley, West Buttress

Jerry Hopfe flew onto Denali on May 2 as a part of the three-member "Steves" team. The group made steady progress arriving at 14,200 feet early on May 11 after camping a night at 13,500 feet. At 0200 on the 12th, the team of three departed the 14,200-foot camp for a summit attempt. When they reached the ridge at 16,200 feet, the full force of the wind made the already frigid temperatures unbearable for Hopfe. Feeling that his hands were close to freezing, Hopfe decided to abort the climb while his partners continued. Hopfe returned to his 14,200-foot camp by 0700 and rested for several hours.

Early afternoon on May 12, Hopfe came to the ranger camp and requested that a medic look at his fingers, which had blistered. Volunteer doctor Jay Mathers evaluated the right hand, which had large blisters on the thumb and first two fingers. Mathers suggested that they take a look at his feet as well. Upon inspection, Mathers discovered that all of Hopfe's toes were blackened and he had moderate trench foot.

Because his teammates had not returned and working a stove would be damaging to his hand, Hopfe remained in the medical tent for the remainder of the day and the evening of the 12th. On the morning of the 13th, eight toes had blistered to the point that only by draining and bandaging them could his boots have been put back on. Hopfe's partners had returned that night as well and were willing to descend with him.

Instead of risking the infection to the toes and further injuring his right hand, it was determined that Hopfe would be evacuated by helicopter. At 1515 Hopfe was evacuated by the NPS Lama helicopter to basecamp, where he was released from NPS care. Hopfe transferred to Talkeetna Air Taxi and returned to Talkeetna.

Hopfe decided to travel to his home in Vancouver, B.C., for his medical treatment. As of the beginning of August his right hand was doing well and expected to make a full recovery. The toes were more seriously injured. While on the mountain, the blebs had formed in a doughnut shape around the first knuckle on each toe. This indicated early on that circulation had not returned to the tips of the toes. Circulation never did return to the eight toes, so doctors removed the tips of each to the first knuckle and today Hopfe has only complete little toes.

Analysis

Frostbite is one of the more preventable injuries in the mountains. In this case, standard daily care, including drying his feet and changing his socks, may have prevented the permanent injury. Hopfe did not have overboots, which may have also helped, but not to the degree that dry socks would have. It is also common knowledge that May is cold, and it is uncommon for climbers to commence a summit bid in the middle of the night. Turning around at 16,200 feet was the best decision that Hopfe made on this ill-fated day. Once the injury occurred, it would have been prudent for Hopfe to seek care immediately so that all extremities could have been aggressively re-warmed in 105-degree F water as opposed to the passive re-warming in the sleeping bag. (Source: Joe Reichert, Ranger)

HAPE, PARTY SEPARTED
Alaska, Mount McKinley, West Buttress

On May 28 at 0745, John Tatzalaff (39) of Team Springer Zissou requested NPS assistance at the 14,200-foot camp because he was experiencing difficulty breathing. A thorough examination by Paramedic Paul Nelson revealed that Tatzalff was experiencing symptoms consistent with High Altitude Pulmonary Edema (HAPE). Tatzalaff presented with crackles in his lower right lobe, tachycardia and a decreased 02 saturation. After consultation with Denali National Park and Preserve physician Dr. Jennifer Dow, Tatzalaff was administered 250mg of Diamox and oxygen at four liters per minute via nasal cannula. Medic Nelson was unable to detect any significant loss of neurological function. After thorough examination and monitoring throughout the day, it was determined, in consultation with Dr. Dow, that Tatzalaff required evacuation.

Though Tatzalaff was a member of a two-person team on his ascent to the 14,200-foot camp, apparently the team of two decided to disband once reaching the 14,200-foot level. Due to the fact that Tatzalaff was now a solo climber on the mountain, he required NPS assistance for evacuation. At 1605, he was evacuated by the NPS helicopter to basecamp at 7,200-feet and transferred to Lifeguard for transport to an Anchorage hospital for further care.

Analysis

Though Tatzalaff ascended at a moderate rate well within accepted norms, he still developed HAPE. Due to sometimes unexplainable circumstances, this happens to even the most experienced climbers. Tatzalaff's lack of climbing with a partner led to the needed intervention and evacuation by the NPS. If Tatzalaff had been climbing with partners, he could have descended with them to a lower elevation with little or no NPS assistance. (Source: John Leonard, Ranger)

(Editor's Note: There were three other altitude-related cases this year, all of them occurring to individuals who had NOT ascended too fast. In one case, the team returned by helicopter to the 7,200-foot level, but the person continued to experience symptoms of AMS.)

OVERDUE CLIMBERS—DISAPPEARED, PROBABLY PERISHED IN A SNOW CAVE FROM HYPOTHERMIA AND/OR ASPHYXIATION, LOST PACK CONTAINING CRITICALLY NEEDED SUPPLIES, WEATHER
Alaska, Mount Foraker, Infinite Spur

Sue Nott (37) and Karen McNeill (37) registered with the National Park Service on March 13th as "Turtle Team" expedition for a climb of the Infinite Spur route on Mount Foraker. Nott checked in at the Talkeetna

Ranger Station on April 19th while Karen McNeill checked in on May 9th. Noted on the check-in form as a rough itinerary were plans to attempt the Moonflower Buttress on Mount Hunter between the dates of April 23 and May 10, followed by the Infinite Spur on Mount Foraker in the period from May 10th to June 8th. The team gave their return date as June 10th. Ranger John Evans noted their intentions to inform basecamp on finer details of their plans. Nott flew to the Southeast Fork of the Kahiltna Glacier on April 23rd. On April 28th Nott and Zoe Heart, who were registered on a separate backcountry itinerary, attempted Deprivation on Mount Hunter. On May 7th Nott and Heart climbed the Mini Moonflower on Mount Hunter. McNeill flew to basecamp on May 9th.

On May 12th Nott and McNeill informed the basecamp manager, Lisa Roderick that they were departing to climb the Infinite Spur on Mount Foraker. Roderick gave them an 'FRS' walkie-talkie-type radio with which to contact basecamp once they were up higher on the route. Nott and McNeill said they would call once able and also told Roderick they were carrying fourteen days of food. Nott and McNeill were also thought to have left basecamp with eight to ten eight-ounce fuel canisters. This information came from subsequent conversations with John Varco, Nott's partner, who had also been at basecamp at the end of April and beginning of May. Nott and McNeill left basecamp on skis for the approach to the route, which travels down the Southeast Fork to the main Kahiltna Glacier where it continues down-glacier, cutting west at a side glacier referred to as the Southwest Fork. The route then traverses a pass referred to as 1st Pass and drops onto an upper arm of the Lacuna Glacier. This is where the pair left their skis, some extra gear, two full fuel canisters, and approximately four days of food. Nott and McNeill then continued over 2nd Pass and onto the Snow Shoulder. This area provides a good view of the route from a relatively safe vantage point. On May 14th Will Mayo and Maxim Turgeon, who were attempting a new route on the South Face of Mount Foraker, made contact with Nott and McNeill. The two teams conversed and then went their separate ways. Mayo later noted that their packs were large, but he had no information on what they were carrying in terms of gear and rations. Mayo also noted that they heard a large avalanche sometime later and checked to see where Nott and McNeill were in relation to it. At that point Mayo did observe them safe at the base of the route. This was the last contact and point last seen of Nott and McNeill.

What occurred in the intervening two-week period, including Nott and McNeill's progress on the route, where they camped, and on what days they were able to move, are unknown. A chronology of the weather as it was observed from basecamp and the 14,200-foot camp on Mount McKinley is summarized below to give some information as to what days may have been conducive to travel. John Varco believes that the pair most likely planned for their ascent to take twelve to fifteen days. At basecamp weather was reasonable with planes able to fly at least part of the day on May 14–16 and May 19. On May 17, 18, and 20, weather was down and no planes were able to reach basecamp. Snowfall was intermittent and fairly minimal and winds were not reported as particularly strong at either basecamp or the 14,200-foot ranger camp. During this first week when Nott and McNeill were on the route, weather was not particularly good, but it is unclear the degree to which weather conditions would have hampered their climbing if at all. For the second week after Nott and McNeill began their climb, conditions continued to be similar from May 21–25, with flights able to get into basecamp. Winds began to increase on May 25th and for the next six days, strong to extremely high winds were reported. The dates of this wind event correspond to the twelfth through fifteenth days that Nott and McNeill were on the route. On May 31st, weather was still marginal. Discussions between Ranger John Evans and staff in Talkeetna began regarding concern over Nott and McNeill's whereabouts. Evans and others at basecamp had been scoping the descent route for several days, but had seen no sign of Nott and McNeill. Also on that day Paul Roderick of Talkeetna Air Taxi called South District Ranger Daryl Miller to express his concern over Nott and McNeill's welfare. Roderick flew the route on May 29 and 30, as well as on at least one other occasion in the prior weeks. Roderick was not able to view the entire route. The portions that were visible to him yielded no evidence of the team other than their approach tracks. On May 29th Will Mayo also flew over the route with pilot David Lee of Talkeetna Air Taxi. Mayo felt he had a good view of the upper half of the route, but saw no evidence of the team. David Lee flew past the route again on May 30th and saw nothing different. In addition, Mark Westman, who climbed the route in 2004, flew over the route on May 21st and saw the same approach tracks leading to and over the bergschrund at the base of the route but nothing above. John Varco was contacted via telephone in the late afternoon of May 31st subsequent to Roderick's phone call to get his assessment of the situation. It was at this point that Varco expressed that he believed it would take the pair twelve to fifteen days to complete the route and the descent. Varco also commented that it was possible for them to stretch their food and fuel as they had done on the Cassin in 2004. Further consideration was given to the situation the following day. At 1700, Chief Sub-district Ranger Daryl Miller made the decision to initiate a search.

On the evening of June 1st, the Lama helicopter, piloted by Jim Hood, made two initial search flights. The first flight with Dave Kreutzer and Mike

Barstat on board searched the Infinite Spur and the intended descent route, the Sultana Ridge, and Mount Crosson from 9,000 to 14,000 feet. Clouds obscured the lower part of the route and the upper part was not searched due to operational restrictions. The second flight with Ranger Meg Perdue on board focused on elevations above 13,000 feet on the route and descent. Possible tracks were observed at the 14,000 to 14,400-foot level traversing onto the Knife Edge Ridge feature of the Infinite Spur. No other evidence of the team was seen on the route or the descent. On June 2nd four flights using the Lama were conducted. Mark Westman and Perdue were on board for the first two flights. On the first flight Westman was able to confirm the tracks that Perdue had seen the previous night as well as identify tracks on sections of the lower part of the route. Westman was confident that he had a good view of the lower parts of the route to 12,000 feet and that Nott and McNeill were not on it. Towards the end of the flight, the debris cones to the west and east of the base of the route were searched. Gear, including a blue and black sleeping bag and a blue and black pack, was seen in the debris cone approximately 100 yards to the east of the start of the route. The sleeping bag was approximately 100 yards west from the pack. No persons were visible or believed to be attached to the gear. It was determined that due to the potential for further avalanche activity, it was unsafe to put personnel on the ground to retrieve the gear or engage in a ground search of the area. On the second flight, possible fall lines consistent with the gear's location were searched, but nothing else was found. At the end of the flight the debris was again searched. A red fleece jacket was also observed 100 yards east of the pack. The third flight used the hydraulic "Grabbers" to retrieve the pack. The pilot is confident that nothing exited the pack while in flight. The pack was later confirmed to be the one carried by Nott. The main compartment and lid pouch of the pack were empty with only a few items, including the FRS radio, in a zipped pocket on the underside of the lid pouch. The pack did have a Ridge Rest sleeping pad still attached with a single strap.

The fading pattern due to the strap's position indicated that the pack was likely lying in that orientation for at least several days prior to its discovery. The pack itself did have several tears, but none so large that it would have been a likely exit route for all the contents. The pack's buckles and straps were undamaged, the hip belt buckle was unfastened, the shoulder straps were relatively loose, and the drawstring on the main compartment was also loose. It did not appear that the pack had been configured for hauling, nor does it seem likely that Nott was wearing it when it fell. On the fourth flight Perdue again searched upper elevations of the route and descent. Photos were taken and nothing new was observed. Flight operations were concluded for that day and Perdue was brought out to Talkeetna to brief the search management team.

On the morning of June 3rd, the search area was segmented and probabilities of area calculated for each search segment. The criteria for probabilities of detection (POD) were based on a pack-sized object and the goal for cumulative PODs set at a minimum of 50 percent. From June 3rd to June 6th, Lama flights and fixed wing aircraft continued to search the Infinite Spur route, potential fall lines from various points on the route and possible descent routes. In total, twenty-seven hours of aerial searching were conducted and the minimum cumulative POD's were achieved for each segment. During this period of the search, hundreds of aerial photos were taken. Based on observations and subsequent photo analysis, tracks were confirmed at the 15,500 to 15,800-foot levels in the Exit Gullies, the 16,400-foot level, and finally the highest likely tracks established at the 16,600-foot level. These upper sections of tracks were on lower angled terrain leading to the south (false) summit, elevation of 16,812 feet. The true, north summit lies a mile beyond this over relatively non-descript terrain. While snow conditions in certain sections could be reasonably expected to retain tracks, no tracks were seen anywhere along the summit plateau though. Also during this same period, observers were placed on the ground at the Snow Shoulder feature to scope the route and call in weather observations to facilitate aerial search activities. While a few possible objects for investigation were seen from this location, none turned out to be anything. Checks were continually made of the debris cone throughout this period to determine if any additional evidence appeared. A brown fleece hat, one glove, a small yellow stuff sack, and a pink wind shell became visible over the course of the search.

Starting on June 7th, the weather precluded search efforts, and through June 14, only one high-level fixed wing flight was possible. As of June 11th, 28 days had passed since Mayo and Turgeon's last sighting of Nott and McNeill at the base of the route. An optimistic estimation would be for a fuel canister to last one-and-a-half to two days, in which case Nott and McNeill would have been out of fuel to make water for seven to ten days. Based on these circumstances, the probability of survival was considered to be extremely low, so the search operation was scaled back. Weather continued to hamper any searching and the next opportunity to fly did not come until June 15th. At that time the Lama was able to search the route to 14,500 feet, but found no new evidence. Nott and McNeill's cache at the base of 2nd Pass was retrieved. This cache was found to contain two fuel canisters and approximately four days of food, thus lessening the food and fuel that the pair was thought to have with them on the route.

On July 9th, the NPS contracted Lama helicopter attempted to fly the search area, but because of high winds moving downward from the summit, it was determined to be an unnecessary high-risk flight. The decision not to fly the upper mountain was made by both the pilot Jim Hood and the helicopter manager Dave Kreutzer. The Lama did fly at approximately 8,000 feet with careful attention given to the debris cones near the bottom of the route. No new evidence was found.

On July 10th, Kreutzer and Hood met with South District Ranger Daryl Miller to express their concerns for the safety of any personnel flying in a search mode, involving hovering up and down the search area, on Mount Foraker. Because of this concern, the fact that there were no signs of Nott and McNeill, aside from the one pack and the tracks that had been found since the search was initiated on June 1st, and that over twenty-eight hours of low-level aerial search had been conducted by the NPS and numerous fixed wing aircraft flights, Miller requested permission from Superintendent Paul Anderson to suspend the search. Anderson agreed with the risk assessment and gave permission to do so.

Analysis

The difficulties of providing an adequate analysis of what transpired in this situation are obvious. With so much left unknown about what exactly occurred, it is only possible, based on the pieces of factual evidence available, to outline possible scenarios and discuss the likelihood of each. The three major issues that can be addressed are 1) the loss of the pack, 2) what happened to Nott and McNeill, and 3) the question of survivability.

How was the pack lost? The pack's location and condition figure heavily into the basis for the following scenarios:

1. *The pack fell over or was blown off the route while sitting on ground.*
Very likely: The relatively undamaged condition of the pack and the gear that was found in its vicinity suggests that Nott and McNeill were taking some sort of break or breaking/setting camp when the pack fell. In addition, extrapolating on where the pack was found, the main fall line leads to two locations at 11,500 feet or 11,800 feet at the start of the Ice Rib. These are two of the prime bivouac sites on the route. Retreat from this location would have been possible, but everyone who knew both climbers agreed that they would have continued the climb, especially if the majority of their fuel and food had not been in the pack at the time of its loss.

2. *The pack fell while being hauled.*
Very unlikely: The pack was not rigged for hauling, the buckles were undamaged and the drawstring closures were undone. The pack's haul loop with carabineer attached was intact and the pack's straps were not cinched down, as would be expected in a hauling configuration.

3. *The pack fell with a climber.*

Very unlikely: The route that the pack would most likely have taken to end up where it was discovered involves multiple falls over steep rock and ice. Any person falling over this terrain would have suffered significant trauma, leaving blood signs on the gear. That the pack was devoid of any visible body fluids negates this theory. In addition, the condition of the pack, including the positioning and lack of damage to the straps and buckles, rules out that it was torn from a falling climber.

What happened to Nott and McNeill? The major piece of evidence that must be considered in framing this discussion is the location and elevation of the tracks seen. There is very little, if any, doubt that the tracks seen on the Infinite Spur route are Nott and McNeill's. The Infinite Spur was last climbed in 2004, while the Talkeetna Spur route on Mount Foraker, which was climbed most recently in 2005 by Nott and Varco, did not show any evidence of their ascent. It is exceedingly unlikely that one route could have held tracks for two years while another route on the same mountain with the same aspect and elevation wouldn't hold them after a year. In addition to the time spent searching, hundreds of photos were studied, and while it is not possible to say with 100 percent certainty that what are believed to be tracks from 16,400 to 16,600 feet are actually tracks, it seems highly likely. Additionally, even into these upper elevations, a careful photographic analysis indicates that most likely the tracks are double, meaning two climbers made them. This suggests that Nott and McNeill essentially made it at least to the top of the route. At that elevation the slope angles are greatly reduced and the difficult sections of the route are accomplished. That no tracks were seen above this point to the false south summit or onto the true north summit nor anywhere down the descent constitutes a pertinent negative. While much of the summit plateau would have not held tracks well, it appeared from the air that snow in at least some places might have held tracks, but none were seen. A number of parties attempted the Sultana Ridge—the descent route—in 2006, but only one of those parties even made it onto the Sultana Ridge itself. This party made it as far as The Way at 11,300 feet, and evidence of their ascent was visible during the search. The potential scenarios as to what happened to Nott and McNeill fall into three main categories: falls (some involving weather), avalanches, and exposure/exhaustion. Each will be considered in turn.

Falling Scenarios:

1. *One Climber (Nott with pack) fell during the first part of the climb.*

Did not occur: Photo analysis of the tracks exiting the Knife-Edge Ridge at 14,600 feet clearly show two distinct sets of tracks. The location of the pack means it is extremely unlikely to have fallen from somewhere other than the "Ice Rib" section of the route between 11,500 and 11,800 feet.

2. *Both climbers fell on the upper portion of the route.*

Did not occur: Analysis of the probable tracks photographed at the 16,600-foot elevation also suggests that two individuals were traveling. The slope angle of this terrain is 30 degrees or less and any fall would not have carried the climbers far and therefore they would have been seen during the search.

3. One or both climbers fell during descent of the Sultana Ridge.

Highly unlikely: The planned descent route was the Sultana Ridge. During the time the climbers would have been descending from the north summit, another climbing party was on the first half of the Sultana and did not see them or evidence of their passing. Examination of the snow and terrain leading to the Sultana did not show any evidence of human passage and tracks would have been found had a person traveled over the area. Following the 25–29th wind event, the descent route and the approach to the north summit was also examined by a spotting scope from basecamp, but no one was seen moving high on the route.

4. One or both climbers fell during descent of an unplanned alternate route.

Highly unlikely: Nott was intimately familiar with the Talkeetna Ridge, having ascended it the year before. This is the closest route to the Infinite Spur and to where their last tracks were seen. Examination of the Talkeetna Ridge did not show any human presence. Footsteps would have been found had someone attempted to descend it. The two climbers were also aware of some existing rappel anchors on the French Ridge immediately to the east of the Infinite Spur. An aerial search of this ridge revealed the footprints of Mayo and Turgeon, but none were seen leading down to the rappel point.

5. Climbers fell into crevasse during ascent or descent.

Unlikely: It is possible that one climber fell into a crevasse, but the possibility that both climbers fell in and were unable to extricate themselves is very unlikely. Both climbers were very experienced with glacier travel and would have been traveling roped together. Had one climber fallen in, the other would be able to aid in extrication and even if that weren't possible, the climber not in the crevasse would have been able to travel and leave additional signs.

6. Climbers were blown off mountain while traveling.

Unlikely: In 2005 Nott climbed Mount Foraker via the Talkeetna Ridge. John Varco, her climbing partner, reported that in 40-mph winds she was forced to crawl along to keep from being blown over. If this had occurred in the location the last tracks were found, the resulting fall would not have been in any way significant. Using 40 mph as the upper limit of wind velocity that the two climbers would have been able to travel in, it can be safely stated that the climbers would not have been lifted up and blown any distance beyond a couple of feet. The fact that Nott was unable to travel in 40-mph winds also eliminates the possibility that both individuals intentionally climbed into the windstorm occurring on the upper reaches of the mountain. The tracks that were found would not have remained after the storm had the two climbers made them during the severe conditions. The tracks would have required time to set to withstand the wind scouring that followed. In addition, at the 14,200-foot camp on Denali, it was noted that tracks made in the preceding days of the storm were still evident afterwards, but areas that people had walked during the storm had been scoured clean. This point supports the theory that the two climbers had reached the 16,600-foot level the evening prior to the storm, because it would have given the resulting tracks time to consolidate. They also would not have been able to reach the highest point where the tracks were last found in any appreciable storm.

7. *Climbers were blown off mountain in their tent during bivouac.*

Possible but unlikely: Had the climbers been bivouacking in the vicinity of the south summit, it is possible to have been rolled off the flat terrain and into one of the couloirs to the southwest of the point the last tracks were seen. However, no evidence that would support this theory was found during the aerial searches.

Exposure/Exhaustion scenarios:

1. *Climbers died from exposure on the surface.*

Highly unlikely: The extensive searches conducted from the helicopter at low altitude and low airspeed would have revealed any human remains on the surface. This would not have been the case with just snowfall, but since the entire summit plateau of the mountain had been scoured by wind, anyone lying on the surface would have been seen.

2. *Climbers perished during storm in a snow cave.*

Likely: The windstorm did not suddenly appear; the onset was over several hours. Had the climbers been in a tent, they would have had ample time to vacate it as the conditions worsened. There are also ample crevasses located in the vicinity of the south summit that would have afforded easy access to shelter.

The likely scenario after taking shelter in a snow cave is that the entrance was covered by drifting snow and the individuals either succumbed to hypothermia (only one sleeping bag and pad was available) or died from asphyxia or carbon monoxide poisoning while they were either asleep or trying to procure water. This would not have occurred early in the storm. It would have been a gradual onset as the storm continued unabated over five to six days. When search operations commenced, neither would have been alive or in any condition to dig themselves out to signal rescue forces.

The question of survivability: The survivability of any of these scenarios is again speculative, but can be discussed in the context of other accidents and their survivability. Falls occurring on technical, steep terrain while occasionally survivable generally cause serious injuries or fatalities, even if initially survivable without immediate help, situations such as this usually soon become fatal. Falls on lower angle terrain or involving a crevasse could have caused an injury that prohibited movement for one or both of the climbers, at which point other factors including weather, lack of equipment or supplies, and exhaustion would contribute to a low survivability over time. An avalanche scenario would have a range of survivability for the initial event, depending on the size of the avalanche, the terrain traveled over, and the distance traveled. Once entrained in debris, survivability drops rapidly after the first thirty minutes, with almost no possibility of survival after twenty-four hours.

A scenario involving exposure or exhaustion would also have a range of survivability, the most critical factor here being the amount of fuel available to melt snow for water. Secondarily, food and equipment available to preserve metabolic capacity would also become factors. As discussed elsewhere in this report, they had fourteen days of food when they left basecamp on May 12th. Approximately four days of food and two fuel canisters were found in the cache at the base of 2nd Pass. This left them with six to eight canisters and ten days of food. Stretching their fuel and using the most optimistic of usage estimates would allow for a canister to last one and a half to two days. Assuming that no canisters were lost with Nott's pack, twelve to sixteen days was the most their fuel could have been expected to last, meaning that sometime between May 25th and May 29th, they would have been out of fuel. Also assuming that no food was lost with the pack and stretching their food half again as many days, they would have exhausted their supplies in that same timeframe. Without water, an individual cannot survive for more than a week. While everyone who knew Nott and McNeill agrees that they had highly developed survival instincts and tremendous will and endurance, there are physiological limitations for all human beings that simply cannot be ignored. While their possibility of survival during the first week in June, during the most intensive part of the search, did exist, that possibility dropped to almost nothing by the time the search was scaled back on June 11th.

Whatever the scenario that Nott and McNeill were involved in, contributing factors to its tragic outcome most definitely include the weather and most likely the loss of Nott's pack during the climb. Such a severe and prolonged wind event as occurred during their second week on the climb would be a test of survival under the best of circumstances. When undertaking difficult, technical routes at high altitude, the margins of safety are often razor thin and such a storm event is extremely likely to have contributed to the fatal outcome in this situation. The loss of equipment is another factor that likely played a role in pushing this situation to its terrible conclusion.

Any piece of gear, particularly a sleeping bag, could be critical to survival when dealing with a situation involving prolonged cold and exposure. The loss of the radio was also tragically unfortunate, as it left no way to contact help if Nott and McNeill were capable of it. The potential fatigue and exhaustion would also be greatly exacerbated by the potentially prolonged period during which the pair was operating with minimal water and food.

As anyone reading this is all too aware, it is unfortunately impossible to know exactly what happened to Sue Nott and Karen McNeill. That will weigh heavily on their family, their friends, and members of the climbing community who wish to make some sense of this accident. The NPS has great confidence, given the amount and character of the searching conducted, that if the pair were visible within the search area, in other words not below the snow's surface either in a crevasse, debris, or a cave, they would have been found. This is certainly part of the basis for assessing the likelihood of each of the scenarios discussed above.

But of course many other factors go into each assessment, the most important being the physical evidence available and the collective knowledge and experience of the dozens of individuals involved in the search as well as the expertise contributed by many members of the climbing community. And while it could be endlessly debated exactly how each piece of information should be weighed and interpreted, ultimately it will not resolve the issue of what happened to these experienced climbers and is only useful to the extent it educates others towards the prevention of accidents in the future. (Source: Meg Purdue, Ranger)

(Editor's Note: This report is included in its entirety in order to demonstrate the level of care and hard work that is put into each search, rescue, and investigation. Special thanks to Daryl Miller, Chief Sub-district Ranger, for his oversight and years of dedication.)

FROSTBITE—INADEQUATE CLOTHING
Alaska, Mount McKinley, West Buttress

On June 2nd, guided expedition AMS-5-Wilkinson departed the 17,200-foot camp on the West Buttress of Mount McKinley for the summit at 0600. This group of six, including two guides, flew to the mountain on May 15th and had made gradual ascent to the 17,200-foot camp in the previous days. The forecasted condition for June 2nd called for cold temperatures and clear skies with moderate winds. During the group's ascent to Denali Pass, member Richard Salter (47) was unable to keep his hands warm. Upon reaching Denali Pass, Salter removed his gloves. His hands appeared pale. Salter alerted AMS guides Wilkinson and Egan to the condition of his hands, Wilkinson and Egan immediately attempted to re-warm Salter's hands by placing them on their warm stomachs and under the armpits of group members. After the attempted re-warming, it was decided that he and Egan would descend to the 14,200-foot camp immediately for further medical attention.

At 1640 on June 2nd, Salter arrived at the 14,200-foot camp and was examined by NPS Patrol Member Richard Hubbard. Hubbard's examination revealed that all digits were cold and mobile with limited sensation, with blue from the tip to between the first and second joint on the first and second fingers and the tips of the third and fourth fingers were blue to the first joint. The right hand exhibited blue to mid-fingers on each of the first three fingers and a pale tip of the fourth finger. Salter's nose was also blue and appeared to be swollen. It was determined through consultation with Denali National Park and Preserve Physician Dr. Jennifer Dow that immediate re-warming of the frostbitten fingers was necessary to mitigate tissue damage. NPS Patrol members Craig Knoche, Paul Nelson, and Hubbard re-warmed and dressed Salter's hands and nose. After re-warming, it was determined that Salter would be unable to descend the mountain and would need to be evacuated by the NPS helicopter.

At 2200, NPS personnel and the14,200-foot camp were contacted by Wilkinson about client Elliot Reed (22). He also appeared to be suffering from significant frostbite to all of his toes. Reed, who had just returned from a successful summit bid, realized while changing into dry socks that he had frostbitten all of his toes. He alerted Wilkinson to his condition. Wilkinson was advised that NPS Ranger John Loomis was to arrive shortly and that he would help in the examination and treatment of Reed. Ranger Loomis confirmed that Reed was suffering from significant frostbite. After consultation with Denali National Park and Preserve Physician Dr. Jennifer Dow and other NPS personnel, it was determined that the best course of action was for Ranger Loomis to try and re-warn the frozen digits at the 17,200-foot camp. Loomis performed a re-warming into the morning hours of June 3. The overall condition of Reed's feet, necessitated his evacuation from the 17,200ft camp.

On the morning of June 3rd, weather conditions allowed for the NPS contract Lama Helicopter to perform the evacuations of both Reed from the 17,200-foot camp and Salter from the 14,200-foot camp.

Analysis

Though the day in which these injuries occurred was colder than average, both of these cases of frostbite could have been prevented. Salter stated that he had cold hands prior to the start of his ascent. He believed that once he got moving, his hands would warm up. Salter also chose to wear gloves instead of the recommended over-mitts. Reed stated that though he had cold feet earlier in the day, he was very surprised to find that he had frostbite later in the day. Reed believed that his feet had warmed up on his ascent; in fact his feet had become numb and then froze. Reed also stated that he had put on an extra pair of thick socks to prevent his feet from becoming cold while attempting the summit. It is probable that the extra socks were detrimental to the warmth of his feet, actually making them colder because of restricted blood flow to his feet. Also, there was a loss of the dead air space that acts as insulation inside of boot liners.

It is important to note that in both of these cases where the clients of a guided trip suffered significant injuries, it is very probable that something as simple as saying, "My hands and feet are cold," to either of their guides would have prevented or lessened these injuries. (Source: John Leonard, Ranger)

(Editor's Note: A few days later, there was another case of frostbitten fingers. The climber attempted to re-warm her fingers near the open flame of a cook stove, which compounded the injury. Medical personnel advocate that the best remedy is skin to skin contact or immersion in 104 degree F water until more advanced care is available.)

FUEL BOTTLE EXPLOSION IN TENT—BURNS
Alaska, Mount McKinley, West Buttress

On June 16, Steve Whitney (34) and Ben Krasnow (29), Alpine Ascents International Guides, were cooking dinner for their clients at basecamp when one of the two MSR Whisperlite stoves experienced an O-ring failure, causing the fuel bottle to explode. One of the guides bent down and attempted to slap the stove away from them when it exploded, causing a fireball estimated to be a minimum of five feet in diameter.

The two received various second-degree burns to their hands and faces. They were treated by cooling using gauze soaked with normal (I.V.) saline solution, then gel burn pads. There was concern that inhalation injuries may have occurred as well. Weather conditions prevented the helicopter from flying. They were evacuated the next day by fixed wing aircraft, having been carefully monitored all night.

Analysis

The guides stated they had had some previous problems with the same pump leaking, so had taken precautions to ensure it was on tight. It can be hypothesized that the two stoves were too close together, causing one pump to overheat and fail.

The group was very fortunate to have only two people injured and to have the accident occur at basecamp where medical treatment could be administered under relatively controlled conditions, and where other guides could take over the supervision of the clients. Enough praise cannot be given to the other mountaineering guides for their unhesitating response both in medical treatment and supervision, which freed this ranger to supervise the medical care and coordinate evacuation plans. (Source: Edited from a report by John Loomis, Ranger)

FALL ON ICE—FAULTY USE OF CRAMPONS, CLIMBING UNROPED, INADEQUATE EQUIPMENT, NO HARD HAT, INEXPERIENCE
Alaska, Chugach National Forest, Byron Glacier

On September 25th at 1815, Alaska State Troopers notified the Alaska Mountain Rescue Group (AMRG) requested assistance for J. Roggenkamp (27), who was wedged in a crevasse on Byron Glacier. According to the subject's climbing partner R. Morill, the pair had been climbing unroped up a prominent ice ramp on the left-center portion of lower Bryon Glacier to the area just below some seracs and ice caves near the 1500-foot level.

The average angle of the glacier in this area is estimated to be 15–20 degrees, but the ridge/ramp they ascended averages 25–35 degrees lower down and falls off 40-45 degrees to the east and west sides. The glacier surface at this elevation and at this time of year is polished blue ice with considerable water running along the surface due to melting.

According to the initial interview on scene with Morill, the pair had just started to descend the glacier via the same ramp they ascended (unroped) when Roggenkamp (who was to Morill's right) tripped by catching a crampon point on his pant leg, fell down and began sliding down the glacier to the north. Roggenkamp attempted to self-arrest, but was unable to and he quickly accelerated down the glacier. Roggenkamp's ice ax was not found, but Morill did have an ice ax. Roggenkamp slid 150–200 feet down the ice ridge to the north/northeast and into the nearest crevasse, wedging feet-first into a moulin up to his shoulders, approximately 30 feet down from the surface of the glacier. Morill descended on the glacier, located Roggenkamp visually, and made voice contact with him from above. According to Morill, Roggenkamp could talk, and indicated he was "all scratched up" and had injured his face, but was "ok." (Roggenkamp had actually sustained a severe head injury, which Morill could not see from above). Morill was unable to lower himself down to Roggenkamp nor to assist him out of the moulin, as he did not have a rope. Morill told Roggenkamp he was going for help and began descending the glacier, arriving at the USFS Begich Boggs visitor center, approximately 2.25 miles away, around 1800 when the Alaska State Police office was contacted. Morill eventually returned to the trailhead and re-ascended to the location of the accident arriving about the same time as the first AMRG rope team around 2000.

Upon arriving at the crevasse, the first AMRG rescuers attempted to make voice contact with Roggenkamp while setting up to lower into the crevasse, but he was unresponsive. After lowering two rescuers into the crevasse and upper part of the moulin, rescuers found the subject to have sustained a severe head injury and to have no carotid pulse.

The eight rescuers on scene prepared a hauling system and extricated the subject from the moulin to the surface, where a second assessment was conducted by an RN and EMTII, who found no signs of life. At this point it was 2315 and the site commander determined that it was unduly risky to the team to attempt to lower the body down the steep glacier in the dark. The priorities of the mission shifted to escorting Mr. Morill off the glacier and getting the AMRG teams out safely. The AST trooper on scene concurred.

Roggenkamp's body was padded and secured to the glacier for retrieval the next day. A fixed line down the glacier was established for safely getting Morill and all rescuers off the glacier and back to the LZ. Morill was escorted down and across the glacier to the LZ by two AMRG members. All field personnel safely traversed to the LZ and were flown to base by the R44 AST helicopter. On September 26, Roggenkamp's body was flown out.

Analysis

Lack of experience combined with inadequate footwear, poor and/or improperly affixed crampons, and descending without protection were the primary factors leading to this accident. In addition, it appears neither of them was carrying a rope or other climbing equipment such as harness, ice screws, etc. Mr. Roggenkamp had inadequate footwear for cramponing on blue ice. When Mr. Roggenkamp's body was pulled out of the moulin, he was only wearing light, trail hiking boots. No crampons were attached.

Such footwear generally does not provide sufficient ankle support and control when traveling on medium-angled glacier ice (particularly on descent), and were generally not designed for attaching crampons. We were told by Mr. Morill that Mr. Roggenkamp had crampons on at the time of the fall, but since they were missing from his feet at the time of recovery, it is uncertain how they were actually affixed to his boots. We do know that it would have been impossible for Mr. Roggenkamp to ascend the polished glacier ice to the location from which he fell without wearing crampons. On the day of body recovery, a single crampon (a 15+-year-old, 12-point strap-on model with one leather strap improperly laced) was found at the second LZ near a pair of tennis shoes and a water bottle.

We believe Mr. Morill may have salvaged this crampon from the accident scene or somewhere on the glacier, but that Mr. Roggenkamp probably wore it, since Mr. Morill wore plastic boots and step-in crampons on his feet the night of the accident. The crampon that was found was still laced, but was missing one of its leather straps and thus was laced incorrectly. It is our conclusion that both of these footwear factors—inappropriate boots and old, poorly laced crampons—may have contributed to Mr. Roggenkamp's fall.

Due to the potential for a significant fall and the obvious crevasse/moulin hazards on this section of the glacier, it was clear to the rescuers that while possible, descending this section unroped involved a high degree of risk of injury or death should a fall occur. Had Mr. Roggenkamp not sustained such severe injuries as a result of his fall, his life would have been jeopardized in another way. Being trapped in a moulin with his entire body in direct contact with the ice and with icy water flowing onto him, he would have become severely hypothermic within a very short period of time and could also have died of exposure before rescuers arrived to extricate him. (Source: Edited from a report submitted by Bill Romberg, Alaska Mountain Rescue Group)

FALL ON ROCK—PROTECTION PULLED OUT, NO HARD HAT
California, Joshua Tree National Park, Spider Line

On January 15, Daniel Scott (26) was climbing Spider Line (5.11c) when one his anchors pulled out causing him to fall twelve feet. According to one posting on SuperTopo, Scott had hung on this piece of protection three or four times before going for the critical move.

Analysis

Daniel Scott was an experienced and careful climber, according to all postings. It is believed that if he had worn a helmet, he would have survived. (Source: From postings in www.supertopo.com)

(Editor's Note: There were many postings regarding this accident, including an obituary from Scott's hometown newspaper in Pittsburg. There is always a deeply personal side to all the narratives found in ANAM, and this one is no exception.)

FALL ON ROCK, CLIMBING ALONE AND UNROPED, WIND
California, Tahquitz Rock

On January 24, Nathan Thomas Parrish's (25) body was found at the base of South Face of Tahquitz Rock between Open Book and Left Ski Track.

Jim Russell, U.S. Forest Service partnership coordinator and two companions found the body and reported it. "Between the two climbs, I discovered a young man's body… his pack, hiking shoes, and sweaters were at the base of the Open Book, so it appears he was free-soloing the climb and fell from high up. I was out bouldering on Monday afternoon and it was VERY windy, so maybe a gust of wind knocked him off balance from one of the upper pitches," according to Jim Russell. (Source: From a report on the www.supertopo.com Climber's Forum)

RAPPEL ERROR–FALL ON ROCK
California, Owens River Gorge, China Wall

On February 4, Ian Seevers Mack (23) died after falling 115 feet while climbing China Wall.

Apparently Mack was preparing to rappel when he fell. Mack was anchored and as his partner was preparing to take a photo, Mack suddenly fell. Climbers nearby reported hearing the call, "Off belay!" They responded with a rescue litter to help get Mack to safety. Sadly, his injuries proved too severe and he later died at the hospital. (Source: Edited from an article in *The Inyo Register*)

FALL ON ROCK, RAPPEL ERROR–FAILURE TO EQUALIZE ENDS OF RAPPEL ROPE, AND FAILURE TO TIE KNOTS IN THE END
California, Joshua Tree National Park, Solid Gold

On February 8, Jay Fitzgerald (21) and Victor Guzik (21 were simul-rappelling off of the second rappel of "Solid Gold" in the Wonderland of Rocks when this accident occurred. The climbers incorrectly equalized the ends of the rope for the rappel, causing one end to remain 30 feet off the ground, though the climbers did not notice it, as the slope of the climb hid the ground from view. Both began the rappel with the climber on the longer end of the rope going first. When Fitzgerald reached the end of the rope 30 feet above the ground, he began to fall toward the ground, causing the rope to slide through the anchor and Victor Guzik to fall ten feet. Fitzgerald hit the ground on his left side suffering the aforementioned injuries. (NB: unspecified fractures). The forest service was alerted and paramedics arrived within three hours and an airlift was made after four hours. Fitzgerald has made a full recovery.

Analysis

Always tie knots in the end of your rappel rope, even when rappelling to the ground (and especially) if the ground is not visible from your anchor. Do not rely solely on the factory printed middle marks as sometimes dirty/darkened spots may be confused with them. Do not simul-rappel simply to save a little time. (Source: Edited slightly from a report submitted by Jay Fitzgerald)

FALL ON SNOW/ICE, CLIMBING ALONE
California, Mount Shasta, Casaval Ridge

On April 28, an experienced young man (17) was climbing alone to train for a Denali climb this season. He fell while down-climbing in loose rocks on Casaval Ridge about 11,000 feet at 0345. He slid on snow/ice approximately 50 vertical feet on a 40-degree slope. A nearby party of three heard him yell and saw sparks when he hit rocks. They were WFR trained and responded, finding a two-inch laceration below his helmet and above his ear. There was no loss of consciousness and the victim remained alert and oriented. However, he was a bit flustered and a concussion was suspected, so the team assisted him descending to their high camp at 9,600 feet. After resting there, they continued to assist him to the trailhead and eventually to Mercy Medical Center.

Analysis

A good reason not to climb alone. A side note: This was a great case of the type of climber camaraderie which should always exist. A trained group gave up their summit plans to assist another climber in need. (Source: Mount Shasta Wilderness Climbing Ranger Report prepared by Eric White, Climbing Ranger/Avalanche Specialist)

FALL ON SNOW/ICE, UNABLE TO SELF-ARREST, INEXPERIENCE
California, Mount Shasta, Avalanche Gulch

On June 3 at 0750, a man (41) fell on snow/ice while ascending at approximately 12,500 feet at the base of the Red Banks in Avalanche Gulch. He attempted to self-arrest but was unsuccessful and fell/slid 1,100 vertical feet. During the fall, his left crampon caught, resulting in fracturing and dislocating his left leg and ankle and multiple bruises and abrasions on much of his body.

A nearby guide observed the fall and called 911. Climbing rangers from Helen Lake (10,400 feet) were notified and responded, arriving at 0845. The climbing rangers and guide stabilized the injured leg and began lowering the victim in a SKED. On a lower angle slope at 11,000 feet, two other climbing rangers arrived at 1130 with a break-down toboggan. The injury was evaluated again. The leg was deformed and out of alignment and his circulation was becoming compromised due to swelling. Helicopter evacuation would be delayed and it was decided that it would be faster to sled the victim to the trailhead, then transported to the ground ambulance and taken to Mercy Medical Center.

He suffered multiple fractures in the leg/ankle area along with dislocation at the ankle. He had emergency surgery that evening and later surgeries to repair the ankle joint. He spent several months recovering and is learning to walk again.

Analysis

The victim had little mountaineering experience, but he was using appropriate clothing and equipment, including a helmet. (Source: Mount Shasta Wilderness Climbing Ranger Report prepared by Eric White, Climbing Ranger/Avalanche Specialist)

RAPPEL ERROR—ROPES UNEVEN, FALL ON ROCK
California, Yosemite National Park, Arch Rock

On June 9, Megan Polk, (27) and Brian O'Day hiked up to Anticipation, a short 5.11b climb at Arch Rock. They climbed the initial 5.9 pitch (about 50 feet) to a small ledge and set up an anchor at the start of the 90-foot 5.11 pitch, a few feet left of the rappel anchors that lead back to the ground.

O'Day led the 5.11 pitch with a 70-meter rope. Polk followed and they rapped back to the start of the pitch. Then O'Day top-roped the pitch, returned to the ledge, and then Polk top-roped it. At the top she clipped to the anchor, untied from the rope, fed it through the rappel anchor, and set up her rappel. As she started down, she noticed over her shoulder what seemed like a lot of rope piled on the ledge below. This raised the possibility that she might not have pulled enough rope through the anchor for both ends to reach the ledge, but it was only a brief thought. She could see the anchor below and feels that perhaps she was fooled by her depth perception as she looked straight down along the wall.

At the bottom of the pitch, O'Day was adjusting their belay anchor in preparation for descending to the ground when he looked up and saw that one end of Polk's rope was about five feet short of the ledge. He shouted to her, but by that time she was so close that it was too late. She rapped off the short end and fell free, 50 feet down the 5.9-pitch below. The rope trailed behind her as the short end pulled through the her rappel anchor, but she fell virtually unrestrained and slammed into the sloping ground at the base, bounced twice, and skidded to a stop, unconscious.

Luckily the end of the rope caught in hardware at O'Day's ledge as it fell past him. He was able to reach it and rappel to Polk. By the time he got to her, she had regained consciousness but was in severe pain and went in and out of consciousness over the next 30 minutes. O'Day immediately ran down to the park entrance station at the base of the talus and phoned for help.

Rescuers began arriving within 20 minutes of the call. They stabilized Polk, short-hauled her from the scene with the park helicopter, and transferred her to an air ambulance for the trip to a trauma center in Modesto. Polk was diagnosed with 12 fractured vertebrae, bilateral scapula fractures, several fractured ribs, three pelvic fractures, a lacerated liver, a ruptured renal artery, and blood in her lungs from pulmonary contusions. She has recovered almost completely and is climbing hard again, but she suffers various residual pains and her left kidney no longer functions. She has no memory of the events from starting her rappel to waking up on the ground. (Source: Keith Lober and John Dill, NPS Rangers)

Analysis

Megan Polk had been climbing about four years and had led trad 5.11b routes. Her partner was experienced enough to lead this 5.11b climb. Both were experienced enough to know about proper rappel set-ups.

In an interview, Polk stated that she seldom ties stopper knots in the ends of rappel ropes. In this case, she also chose not to use an autoblock system. Many climbers will forego this because the situation seems so "simple."

The 70-meter rope was more than long enough. Polk was responsible for verifying that both ends reached the belay, first by asking O'Day, second by checking during the descent. We are also reminded that partners should check each other's rigging whenever possible. Unfortunately, her memory of what she thought and did (or didn't do) on the rest of the rappel was wiped out by the blow to her head.

It's obvious that Polk was extremely lucky, given her injuries and the fact that she was not wearing a helmet. The steep dirt/rock slope may have helped cushion the blow, but one rock in the wrong place could have killed her. (Source: John Dill, NPS Ranger, and Jed Williamson)

STRANDED—ROPES STUCK IN CRACK, INADEQUATE CLOTHING, EQUIPMENT AND FOOD, FATIGUE
California, Yosemite National Park, Fairview Dome

At 2048 on August 13, Matt Ciancio was solo climbing the regular route on Fairview Dome when he heard cries for help. Ciancio stopped midway up the route to investigate. He made verbal contact with two climbers. They told him that their ropes were stuck in a crack, that they were unable to continue, and that they needed a rescue. Ciancio topped out on the regular route and came to the SAR campsite in Tuolumne Meadows campground to report the incident. The SAR response was initiated.

At 2130, SAR members Roberts and Clayton hiked to the base of Fairview Dome and made contact with the stranded climbers, Andre Colmenares (23) and David Allfrey (21), who stated that they were in between pitches 7 and 8. They had no warm clothes, no headlamps, no food or water, and were too tired to continue. They needed assistance.

Around 2300, Roberts and Clayton arrived on top of Fairview to spot the focal point, fall line, and rigging site for the operation. This was done with assistance from Ranger Lawler on the Tioga Rd. Through his patrol car, he made contact with Colmenares and Allfrey. He had the climbers flash their cigarette lighter in order to locate them on the rock face. By radio, he and Roberts were able to get an exact location on the summit of the focal point. At 0030, all SAR personnel, including Ranger Ramsdell, were on top and beginning rigging for a high-angle rescue. All ropes were rigged and ready for operations by 0155.

Adhering to NPS protocols, a main line and a belay line were implemented. Roberts was lowered over the edge to locate and make contact. He was then lowered about 400 feet to their position on a small three-foot by six-foot ledge. Colmenares and Allfrey said they were very cold, dehydrated, and hungry. Roberts provided them with warm clothes, food, and drink. They were uninjured and in a fairly good mood.

Being properly secured to the ropes by Roberts, Colmenares and Allfrey jumared one-at-a-time to the top. This was accomplished by jumaring the main line while they were being belayed on the line from above. Both were on top and clear of the ledge by 0332. Roberts cleaned the anchor on the rock face and also jumared to the top on belay. He was clear of the edge by 0408. The rigging team demobilized all anchors and ropes and was ready to hike out by 0425. The team and climbers hiked down the back side of Fairview together. Everyone was back at the SAR Cache by 0545.

Analysis

Around 0545, I talked with David Allfrey about the incident. Allfrey said that he and his partner began climbing the Inverted Staircase around 1030 on August 13. Both climbers had done the regular route on Fairview earlier in the year and felt they were up for the challenge of this route. Both have less than two years climbing experience. (Source: Edited from a report by Ted Roberts, Search and Rescue Technician)

FALL ON ROCK, POSITION—FACING OUT DOWN-CLIMBING SLABS
California, Yosemite National Park, Lembert Dome

On August 14, Aaron Barnett (19) and Dustin Holcomb (21) were going to climb the NW Books (5.6) on Lembert Dome. Holcomb had led it before and would lead today. The approach to many of the routes in this area, including the NW Books, involve 2nd and 3rd class slabs. Barnett and Holcomb were deliberately off route exploring the area when they decided to descend to the base to make the approach to their intended climbing route. They were taking slightly separate routes down the slabs when Barnett slipped and slid about 100 feet. His left foot hit a crack and spun him around, fracturing his ankle and twisting his foot almost 90 degrees to one side.

Holcomb hiked out to tell the NPS about the accident. The SAR team reached Barnett about thirty minutes later and carried him to the ambulance for transfer to Mammoth Hospital.

Analysis

Both had plenty of experience peak bagging and were comfortable on normal 3rd class. They were both ski and snowboard instructors and comfortable in out-of-bounds terrain in those sports. They had skied or snowboarded on Mount Shasta—couloirs, etc. Barnett had less climbing experience. He had followed a couple of trad routes but did not lead.

Barnett and Holcomb were wearing rock shoes and both felt comfortable on the slabs. They had not found themselves in over their heads looking for a way out. Holcomb thinks Barnett may have fallen because he was facing out and wearing a pack, which could have put his weight too far back for good friction. Holcomb had his helmet in his pack. He doesn't remember if Barnett had a helmet with him but doesn't think he was wearing one at the time.

Barnett's ankle has healed well. He is skiing and climbing again. (Source: Ted Roberts, Search and Rescue Technician, and John Dill, NPS Ranger)

STRANDED, OFF-ROUTE, INADEQUATE CLOTHING AND EQUIPMENT, EXCEEDING ABILITIES, WEATHER
California, Inyo National Forest, Mount Ritter

On September 7th, the park received a mutual aid request from Mono County SAR for assistance in rescuing a stranded climbing party on Mount Ritter, a few miles southeast of the park. On Thursday, five men between the ages of 15 and 21 reached the summit of the mountain (13,157 feet) without resorting to technical climbing. While descending, though, they were hit by a storm with sleet and snow. They became disoriented and down-climbed off-route into highly technical terrain. Without technical gear and with inadequate clothing, they were forced to huddle together at about 12,500 feet through the night. Eventually they called the Mono County Sheriff's Office by cellphone, and the county contacted the park. A rescue team comprised of Yosemite heli-tack crew members Eric Small, Nick Fowler and John DeMay, Valley District ranger Jack Hoeflich, and Mather District rangers Eric Gabriel and Jason Ramsdell flew to the area in the park helicopter, piloted by Dave Boden.

The stranded climbers were spotted from the air on the north face of the peak in fifth class terrain. Rescuers were short-hauled under the helicopter onto the wall and the stranded party rigged for evacuation. In three separate flights, all of the climbers and rescuers were safely short-hauled off the peak to a meadow at the base of the mountain. The climbers were wet, cold, and dehydrated, but were able to walk back to their campsite. Given the weather, temperatures, and lack of warm clothing, the outcome could have been more serious had they been forced to spend another night on the wall. (Source: From a report by Jason Ramsdell, Mather District SAR Coordinator)

(Editor's Note: While not a climbing accident, this narrative is presented as an example of hikers finding themselves in a climbing situation for which they were not prepared or capable of handling.)

FALL ON ROCK, FAILURE TO FOLLOW INSTINCTS—NOT TO CLIMB THAT DAY
California, Yosemite National Park, Low Profile Dome

At 1630 on September 8, Ranger Mike Yost received a call at the Tuolumne Meadows Ranger Station regarding an injured climber at the base of Low Profile Dome. The report came from a credible local climber, Peter Croft, who said he watched a woman fall from the route Shit Hooks and hit the ground and that her left lower leg was deformed with an open fracture.

At this time a page was sent out for additional SAR personnel. Within minutes a technical carry-out team was formed and dispatched to the scene. At the base of the Low Profile Dome, they found Anna Siebelink (44) supine, covered in jackets and with climbers helping hold the injured leg/ankle. Paramedic Colflesh began medical treatment, starting IV's and administered morphine for pain, per Yosemite Clinic. He splinted the lower leg and prepared the patient for the litter out.

At 1740, a technical lowering of Siebelink was started. A belay line was put in place with rock protection. She was lowered 15 feet to the trail where she was then littered out to the road and taken in the Tuolumne ambulance to May Lake. She was flown from there to Memorial Hospital in Modesto.

Analysis

The leader, Andrew Statesberry, was belaying from above and was unable to see his partner. The climbing rope coming from Siebelink lodged itself in a flake directly above her. The leader was pulling the rope in, but because it was stuck in the flake, a loop of slack had formed.

One of the main points that I get from this accident is that a short, seemingly harmless fall can cause a significant injury. (Source: Edited from a report by Ted Roberts, Search and Rescue Technician, with the last sentence being added by John Dill, Ranger)

Two letters (slightly edited) from Anna Sieblank shed some additional light:

I have been climbing since 1989, leading and following all over the west coast, Yosemite, J-tree, Eastern Sierra, Palisades, Tahoe, etc. I lead 5.9 —and some 5.10—trad and sport routes comfortably 5.9 and follow up to 5.11. I am primarily an outdoor trad climber and very rarely boulder. The person I was climbing with was someone I had met recently. He is also an experienced climber and guide in England. I would say my impression is that he is very competent and experienced.

I am now after eight months re-habing well, I had a non-union of the bone, which took awhile. I am back to hiking three miles with a cane, riding a bike on flats and hoping to climb soon. I am still limited by range of motion and pain but getting better.

What are the lessons from this? If your first thought late afternoon is to sit by the river and have a beer, you should follow that instinct, but IF you do get injured, do it in a place where a ton of handsome rescuers come out of the woods to rescue a damsel in distress!

In addition to paying attention to instinct, I do think there are some valuable points to learn from in regards to when I actually did the climb…

…I do not really feel that the rope was stuck. It was more like I was guiding and redirecting the rope.

If I had five seconds to turn back, I would pay attention to all those things that came up just before starting the climb. The climbers I was with had done everything correctly. What I noted were some simple things that I could have changed at the bottom before starting the climb. The rope was not quite back-clipped at the right angle, the rope was slack and maybe I should yell "Up rope!" or ask for a spot. Nah, no big deal, I'll just head up quickly, I thought. Well, I really should have listened to that gut feeling. Sure, it still could have happened, but it's a good lesson in paying attention to your intuition.

(This route) is known for its awkward first funky move right off the deck, a lie-back. I started the climb in the lie-back position and made a move, then, to get the rope around the flake, leaned forward and took a hand off to redirect the rope. The hand off and forward shift caused my left foot to slip and come off.

(Editor's Note: Thanks to Ms. Sieblank for her perspective on the incident.)

FALLING ROCKS—DISLODGED BY CLIMBERS, PARTY SEPARATED, POOR POSITION
California, Mount Shasta, Avalanche Gulch

Two separate parties (totaling four people) were climbing Avalanche Gulch in the poor September conditions (loose rocks, lack of snow). Unfamiliar with the route, they veered off route at 13,000 feet and crossed the open Konwakiton Glacier. Untrained in glacier travel, they were uncomfortable with this route and decided to descend via another route. They chose the West Face, which had even less snow on it than Avalanche Gulch. While descending, one member left, choosing yet another route. The other three continued down the West Face. At 10,200 feet on a 35-degree slope, they left the snow patch, moving to loose rock. They observed both natural and human triggered rock fall and decided to move back to the snow. During that time (1645), they triggered the release of a boulder and other rocks, knocking down two of the climbers and directly hitting the third. All three tumbled 100 feet vertically and 250 feet horizontally. The climber directly hit (30-year-old female) was found by her climbing partners moaning and with difficult breathing. The other climbers had only minor injuries. They called 911 at 1800. The injured climber was assisted by her partners to low angle terrain at 9,200 feet. Two CHP helicopters began to search at 1845. Due to lack of snow, the climbers blended in well with the rocks and were not spotted until 1925. They were evacuated at 1940 hours. They were all flown to Mercy Medical Center. They declined treatment. The injured climber was treated for broken ribs, bruising, and hematoma damage to the chest and shoulder.

Analysis

Mount Shasta consists of 120 cubic miles of loose rock! Even the bedrock outcrops are not to be trusted. Therefore, the best time to climb is when the mountain is predominantly covered with snow and the avalanche danger is low. This usually occurs in the late spring to mid summer. Loose rocks and boulders along with natural rockfall occur every year by mid summer into the fall.

Additionally, group separation is not recommended. The fourth climber descended alone and was not able to help his friends. Keep your group together. You may need their help or they may need you! (Source: Mount Shasta Wilderness Climbing Ranger Report prepared by Eric White, Climbing Ranger/Avalanche Specialist)

FALL ON ROCK, PROTECTION PULLED OUT, INADEQUATE PROTECTION, EXCEEDING ABILITIES
California, Yosemite National Park, Cathedral Peak

Cathedral Peak South East Buttress is a popular six-pitch moderate alpine climb, with many variations, about 3.5 miles from the road, at around the 10,500-foot elevation. This incident involved a party of three climbers, Dave Lubertozzi (42), Sumi Nadarajah (30), and Mike Ray (40), who started climbing the "middle" variation and moved over to the right. By around 3:15 p.m. on September 30, they were climbing the third pitch, about 300 feet from the base of the climb. The leader, Dave, fell ten feet above his last piece while trying to make the next placement. He was at the "5.6 fingers over bulge" marked just below the third belay station for route C in the SuperTopo. After falling vertically with his left foot tangled in the rope, he was yanked hard by the ankle. The piece of protection pulled out and he tumbled onto a sloping ledge, where he lay disoriented for about 30 seconds. He began to move and told the other climbers he was "basically OK except for the ankle", which he thought was broken. Another climbing party also on the route saw the fall, but didn't inquire as to whether they needed help, and climbed on, but then the injured climber and his party didn't ask them for help either. Sumi tried to call friends back at camp from her Verizon cellphone, but only got voice mail; they decided not to call YOSAR, thinking it was early and they could still get out on their own.

Mike, who was belaying, lowered Dave to their anchor, tied the double ropes together and they began to rap the route. Dave rappelled going face-out, feet-first, using an autoblock. On each rappel, Mike descended first and chose the next anchor, Dave descended next, and Sumi came down last so that Dave had help at both ends of the rappel, and a fireman's belay from below. One of the ropes was damaged to the core during the fall, so they isolated the bad spot with a butterfly knot. Since it was near one end, with good planning they were able to make it down in two short and one long rappels which necessitated passing the knot only once.

Sumi attended to Dave, making a crude splint with sticks, dressing him in warm clothing, and giving food, water, and 800mg ibuprofen while Mike got down the ropes and as much gear as safely possible. Then they descended another ~200 feet of scree, Dave sliding on his butt with assistance from the others. They decided to head west towards the JMT rather than back along the Budd Creek approach. After reaching the relatively flat saddle area, they tried various means of locomotion for the injured climber: three-legged hop with one or both of the others supporting his shoulders, with a crutch, crab-walk, trying to carry him once on Mike's back, and again with a carrier woven from the rope. But he was too heavy to take very far and he couldn't take the pain of hopping. They were about a mile from the trail, which was then another ~3 mi to the car, so they figured they'd try to get to the trail where they might meet someone. Around 8:30 p.m. it was getting pretty dark, so they decided Mike would run back by himself to go for help while the others continued on towards the trail. By this time Dave had decided the most efficient way to move was by crawling, so they made him some knee pads and put the foot up in a sling so it didn't drag. It was pretty slow going. They stopped and he had a snack and some water while Sumi scouted out for the trail ahead. She reported it looked like they were going to have to go downhill over rough terrain and through some trees to get to it, so they decided to hunker down and wait for rescuers there.

They were approximately 300 yards from the trail at the edge of the large clearing and still around 10,000 feet. It was windy there but they figured it would be easier for them to be seen out in the open rather than in the woods. This was about 10:00 p.m. and it was starting to get really cold with a few flakes of snow falling. There was one space blanket. It was the sleeping bag type, so they split it to share it but it got kind of shredded in the wind. They used it and the tarp, ropes, and backpacks and made a nest as cozy as they could between two small trees and cuddled up in there and shivered until about 2:00 a.m. when their friends came.

Back at camp at the end of their day, the rest of the group expected to find the three climbers who went to Cathedral Peak back already, since they had left at 6:00 a.m. They figured they were just being slow, but began to really worry around 10:00 p.m. Some of them wanted to hike up the trail to find them. In discussing it, the group decided that even if there were something wrong, they'd have a hard time finding them and couldn't really know what kind of help they needed anyway, so couldn't bring proper/useful gear, so should just stay put and wait.

At 10:50 p.m., one of the three missing climbers (Mike) drove into camp and said, "We have an incident..." The group began discussing options, and Val (a former SAR volunteer) was for immediately sending out a crew with tents/sleeping bags/stove/first aid gear while others favored contacting YOSAR first. A few raindrops falling decided for immediate action. At 11:15 p.m., four of them, Brian, Matt, Mike and Cheryl (a Wilderness EMT) headed out with six sleeping bags, two tents, a few pads, food, water, iodine, a stove, and an FRS radio, while the others called YOSAR.

They left the Cathedral Lakes trailhead about 11:45 p.m. and got to the neighborhood of the JMT below the saddle around 1:30 a.m. After leaving a note on the trail for YOSAR in a Ziploc bag on a cairn, with rock-and-stick arrows, they fanned out about 100 meters apart, and headed generally up. One set of lights appeared on the trail and the rescue party met the second group of climbers on their way out, but they had no information about their friends. As they continued, they saw another set of lights coming up the trail behind them, so three waited thinking it might be YOSAR. Brian ditched his pack and went up the hill as fast as he could, then spotted his friends' lights. He sprinted over to within earshot, yelled to them who it was and that he had others to guide back. He asked if they needed anything immediately. They said no immediate help was needed, so he dashed back to the crew and they headed on up, reaching Sumi and Dave around 2:15 a.m.

The rescue crew basically set up a field hospital, and within a half hour, Dave and Sumi were warm and stable in tents with pads and sleeping bags, and Cheryl (EMT) had looked at and re-splinted Dave's ankle, checked out his other injuries, recorded vitals, and gave a (fourth) dose of ibuprofen (800 mg) plus 50 mg diphenhydramine. She stayed with him until YOSAR came. At about 4:00 a.m. they all went to bed, leaving Brian on watch for YOSAR. Brian also hiked down to modify the YOSAR note to explain the location of the camp better.

YOSAR meanwhile had gone up the Budd Creek approach and scouted all around the base before bedding down. They arrived about 7:00 a.m., verified that the EMT had done a thorough job, and put Dave on oxygen and a spine and back stiffener, as there was evidence of a possible c-spine injury. After being diverted by a fire at Hetch Hetchy, the helicopter came about 11 a.m. and flew Dave to Mammoth Lakes with a YNP medic.

Analysis

The proximate cause was that I slipped off my foothold while trying to re-do a cam placement I wasn't happy with after I first placed it. The next piece down (a nut), I also wasn't happy with, blew on the way down, so I took up to a 40-foot fall, probably less as I came to rest on a low angle patch of ledges, kind of like stairs.

Thinking about it for the last few days it's obvious that a lot of bad decisions came together to create the accident. The first was that as a new leader, it would have been better to do something a lot closer to the road in case anything happened. Secondly, after making some placement mistakes on my first pitch, I meant to pay special attention to pro, and after four nice pieces was feeling more confident...too much so. I didn't like the fifth piece, a small nut, but barreled on ahead anyway, thinking it was as good as it was going to get. Later I realized I could have easily backed it up; if the rock there only allowed a marginal piece, then two or three would have made more sense. As I came to near the top of the sequence, there was a bit of a tricky move I wanted to protect, but after that was a huge ledge, so I would be "home free". In fact I started thinking as if I was already there -- dumb. Why I didn't just clip the cam I had in I'll never understand. Really dumb. It may not have been an award-winning placement, but it was 1) right at my chest and 2) a lot better than the nut ten feet below me! I'll never get the image out of my mind of falling off with the friggin' cam in my hand, lobes retracted, as I just pulled it out of a perfectly good crack! The fall itself was pure carelessness. Although my left toe was on a huge bomber crystal, it was on the face outside of the half-pipe my body was in, with the crack at the back right, so in fact I forgot where my center of mass should be since I felt protected with my body in the rock groove; when I leaned in to get a better shot at the cam placement, I un-weighted the left foot a bit (which was my only real hold) and off I came.

Finally, I probably wouldn't have broken my ankle if I hadn't purposely put the rope outside the groove to my left instead of between my legs where it belonged, since the crack was vertical. Dumb! Ultimately a lot of my attitude had to do with recently having gotten over my fear of falling since I'd started climbing, as the consequences of falling on toprope are minimal. I simply wasn't being careful enough on lead. I'm really glad no one else got hurt. (Source: Edited slightly from a report submitted by Brian Welsh, Mike Ray, Sumi Nadarajah, and David Lubertozzi, the latter having done the analysis)

(Editor's Note: We always appreciate it when climbers write up their own mishaps and are totally honest in their analyses.)

FALL ON ROCK, PROTECTION PULLED, INADEQUATE PROTECTION
California, Yosemite Valley, El Capitan, Salathé Wall

On October 13, Martin Klinger (26) of Germany was attempting to lead the first pitch of the Salathé Wall on El Capitan. He was with a party of two other climbers from Pennsylvania who intended to climb the Free Blast section of the Salathé Wall. Klinger had met the two other members of the party in Camp 4 approximately one week prior.

Klinger offered to lead the first pitch. He placed a piece of gear about 15 feet up on a ledge and then a second piece, a #2 Camalot, five feet above the ledge. He then climbed about 20 feet of moderate crack to place his third piece—a yellow-green hybrid alien. After placing his third piece, he attempted the crux. On his first attempt, he fell and slid about ten feet down to a stance without weighting the hybrid alien. On his second attempt, he fell again. This time, the hybrid alien pulled and he fell approximately 30 feet down to the ledge, bounced off, and fell another ten feet until being stopped by the rope held by the #2 Camalot. At the end of the fall, he was about ten feet above his belayer. Mr. Klinger suffered trauma to his ankles, back, and head. The belayer, Scott Woods (~30) noted that Klinger experienced a brief loss of consciousness and amnesia.

Woods lowered Klinger to the ground. He was transported by park service personnel—using spinal precautions—to the medical clinic in Yosemite and subsequently transported by helicopter to Fresno for further evaluation. He was discharged from the hospital approximately 36 hours later with the diagnoses of 1) multiple transverse process fractures of the lumbar spine, 2) small subdural hematoma, 3) hematoma of the right psoas (a muscle which lies against the back wall of the lower abdomen and connects the lumbar spine to the femur), 4) facial abrasions, and 5) ligamentous injuries to bilateral ankles.

Analysis

After discussing the accident with Scott Woods, the following observations can be made. Klinger might have greatly reduced his risk of a long fall by placing additional protection at the crux or at least more carefully considering the hybrid alien placement. In retrospect, Woods felt that the green-yellow alien was too small for the crack in which it was placed. Additionally, Klinger was using Wood's rack to climb, so it is possible that he did not know that the piece he placed was a hybrid with two sets of cams of different sizes. After falling on the crux the first time, he should have realized that there was a high probability of a second fall and might have avoided significant injury by placing a second piece of protection.

Because Woods did not know Klinger well, he attributed Klinger's decision to place only one piece of protection at the crux as evidence of his level ability as a climber. Woods felt that if he had known Klinger better, he would probably have suggested that he place additional protection after the first fall occurred. An open channel of communication between the two climbers might have prevented this incident. The lack of familiarity between the belayer and leader and the fact that the leader spoke English as his second language may have made this difficult.

Klinger should also have been wearing a helmet, particularly when climbing at the base of El Capitan during the busiest part of the big-wall climbing season. His intra-abdominal and intra-cranial injuries could easily have been life threatening. (Source: Edited from a report submitted by Tim Platts, Mills, MD, Brian Stork, MD,Fresno, CA, and from Ranger Michael Siler's Case Incident Report)

FALL ON ROCK, RAPPEL ERROR—WORN HARNESS BELAY LOOP BROKE
California, Yosemite Valley, Leaning Tower

On October 23, Todd Skinner (48) and his partner Jim Hewitt were rappelling fixed lines from the Jesus Built My Hotrod route after an attempt at free-climbing it. The belay loop on Skinner's harness broke when his body weighted the system. He fell over 500 feet into the talus at the base of the wall. His GriGri and carabiner were still firmly attached to the rope.

Analysis

Jim Hewitt stated that Skinner was aware that the belay loop was in a deteriorated condition prior to the climb, as he and Skinner had inspected it and discussed its poor condition three days earlier. Hewitt estimated the loop to be twenty percent under strength due to wear. Skinner had said that his new harness was on order but had not arrived yet, so he continued to use the much worn harness. (Source: From a report by Keith Lober, Ranger, Yosemite National Park)

(Editor's Note: It is difficult for the climbing world to understand how Todd Skinner, one of the most experienced climbers in the world, could convince himself to use this harness—or, having decided to use it, not to clip in to the harness waist band as well. Again, as with last year's incident of Jim Ratz rappelling off the end of his rope, we are reminded that no matter our level of experience, none of us is immune from making errors.)

FALL ON ROCK, LOWERING ERROR—LOST CONTROL OF BELAY AND NO KNOT IN END OF ROPE, NO HARD HAT
Colorado, Eldorado Canyon State Park, Rincon

On January 19, James Harr (25) fell to his death when his partner Dave Booton lost control of the climbing rope he was using to lower Harr to the ground. The rope slipped through Booton's belay plate. Harr's fall was 20 feet and he landed on his head. (Source: From an article in the *Rocky Mountain News*)

Analysis

It would appear they didn't know the rock well enough to understand that the best option here might be to rappel rather than lower. Another question is why they didn't have two ropes. It seems that the new generation of climbers takes only one rope on multi-pitch climbs. Taking two ropes, even if the second one is only of small diameter, provides the opportunity to rappel. Whether lowering or rappelling, tying a knot in the end(s) of the rope is usually a good idea. (Source: Jed Williamson)

FALL ON ROCK
Colorado, Black Canyon of the Gunnison, Scenic Journey

On May 17, Craig Smith (21) was leading the eighth pitch of the 13-pitch climb Scenic Journey (5.10+), when he wedged his hand into a crack in the rock face to gain a hold. The move was awkward and he couldn't make it stick. He fell both the ten feet to his protective anchor and the ten feet below it. His rope caught him, but his right foot slammed into the wall with a bone-splintering crunch. Over the next seven hours, the men managed to rappel 1,000 feet.

They reached the canyon floor by 9:00 p.m. and for the next nine hours, Smith crawled up to the canyon rim, wearing his rain gear so he wouldn't get poison ivy. They were both quite dehydrated by the time they were half way up because with no water purifier, they decided not to drink water from the nearby Gunnison River. They were fortunate to find a cave with water dripping over the lip. They were able to drink and fill water bottles.

They got to the rim and campground just about sunrise. Smith noticed park Service sign that said, "Caution, very dangerous. Technical climbers only." (Source: Edited from a story by John Aguilar, *Rocky Mountain News)*

Analysis

It should be noted that they didn't get started until 4:00 p.m. on the 16th because they were trying to find the start of the route. They did four pitches then bivouacked, starting in again the next day.

These climbers are to be commended for successfully rescuing themselves in a remote and difficult place. (Source: Anonymous local climbers)

RAPPEL ERROR—ANCHOR FAILED
Colorado, Boulder Canyon, Boulderado

On June 3 at 1635, the Boulder County Sheriff's Office was advised of a fallen climber in Boulder Canyon. Rocky Mountain Rescue Group, Pridemark Ambulance, Nederland Fire Department, Sugarloaf Fire Department, Boulder County Victim Advocates, the United States Forest Service, and Sheriff's Deputies responded.

At the scene, a man (29) was found on a ledge near the base of a climbing area called the Boulderado. Witnesses said that the climber (29) was setting up a "top-rope" and was seen beginning to rappel from the top of the climb. After he lowered himself about ten feet, the rope anchor failed and he fell about 70–100 feet. During the fall, his rope became tangled in a small tree growing out of the rock face. This stopped his fall about five feet above the ledge. Witnesses cut the rope in order to allow them to lower him to the ground.

From the ledge, the Rocky Mountain Rescue Group conducted a vertical evacuation of about 50 feet to the road. The victim was then transported to a waiting Flight for Life helicopter and was flown to St. Anthony's Central Hospital with serious injuries.

Analysis

The exact mechanism of the rope anchor failure is unknown, however, a rock, weighing an estimated 250 pounds, was found at the top of the climb that had been very recently dislodged. The rock was resting precariously near the edge of the rock face above the climbing area and vehicle traffic below. After the rescue operation was complete and all people and vehicles moved out of the area, the rock was pushed over the edge to eliminate it as a future safety concern. (Source: Edited from a report from the Boulder County Sheriff's Office)

(Editor's Note: This year there were several incidents involving this kind of anchor problem or lowering problem in Eldorado and Boulder Canyon. A few of the typical ones have been reported here. There was also a fatality at Garden of the Gods, but no pertinent details were available.)

FALL ON ROCK, FALLING ROCK—CLIMBER STANDING ON LARGE ROCK WHEN IT CAME LOOSE, CLIMBING UNROPED
Colorado, Little Bear, Northwest Face

On July 2 about 10:00 a.m., an experienced climber died from a fall taken from the upper headwall (just below the Blanca-Little Bear ridge) of the Northwest Face route on Little Bear. The party he was in was not roped at the time. He tried to move on a large rock that appeared to be solid. It came off on top of him. The initial fall was about 20 feet, but he continued to tumble down for about 300-400 feet. He died during the fall/tumble from multiple head contusions (though he was wearing a Petzl Ecrin Rock helmet), severe internal injuries, and severely broken extremities (including neck).

The rescue-turned-recovery operation began almost immediately due to radio communications available in the area. His partners reached him about 20 minutes before assistance arrived. A nurse and an experienced SAR member concurred that he was deceased.

The recovery operation began immediately. The body was lowered 700–800 feet to the scree field below the lower headwall where the county SAR team took over from the climbers. Sleet and rain hampered the operation, in particular over the waterfall in the gully north of the "Black Hand." The body was then driven out by one of the SAR team members. The operation was wrapped up at about 10:00 p.m. His partners were uninjured. (Source: From a report by Theo Barker, SAR member who happened to be nearby. His wife is the nurse mentioned)

FALL ON ROCK, OFF ROUTE, INADEQUATE BELAY
Colorado, Eldorado Canyon State Park, Red Garden Wall

On July 13 a climber (37) took a 100-foot fall on the Red Garden wall in Eldorado Springs before his partner managed to control the rope, stopping his partner's descent about ten feet above a rock ledge. The climber suffered minor head injuries and cuts, Boulder County sheriff's deputies said. He was taken to Boulder Community Hospital.

His climbing partner, Nick Saylor (19), said the man was an experienced climber who slipped after getting off route. Saylor, whose hands were bandaged by rescuers on scene, said he was climbing above his partner and it took him several seconds to stop the rope.

"The rope just went right through my hands," Saylor said. "I guess you can see the bones." Saylor was able to lower his friend to the ledge and yell for help until someone called 911. It took rescuers an hour and 10 minutes to get the climber safely to the ground. (Source: From various postings at the website http://mountainproject.com)

Analysis

The most interesting aspect of this incident has to do with the belay. There are not enough details, but we are seeing more and more incidents having to do with belayers "losing control" of the rope. The lesson is to review the very basics of belay techniques. (Source: Jed Williamson)

FALL ON SNOW, CLIMBING UNROPED, INEXPERIENCED
Colorado, Longs Peak, Lamb's Slide

On August 19, Ben Cort (age unknown) was climbing Lamb's Slide with two friends. When Cort was at the top, he lost his footing and fell some 800 feet. "The next thing you know I was just flying down the mountain without my ice ax," he said. "That's when it gets bad." Traveling at speeds witnesses estimate were near 40 mph, Cort stayed conscious for the entire fall. "Total pandemonium," he said. "I was head over heels and I was smacking my face on rocks. Rocks were coming down with me and then this boulder rolled over me a couple times." When Cort reached the bottom, he initially thought he was dead. "There was a very, very distinct feeling that I knew that that's how I was going to die. I was just sure," he said. "My friends were positive I was dead. I've been climbing long enough and have been around this sport long enough that you take something like that and you know that's kind of it." Remarkably, Cort not only survived, but was left with only a broken leg and shoulder, and some scrapes and cuts. "I hit the ground and I felt my feet, I felt my fingers and was just so overcome with gratitude because I knew that God had just decided to save me," he said. His climbing group, which included a man with Rocky Mountain Search and Rescue, immediately came to his aid. Cort says complete strangers also stopped to help him. "It was hailing. It was raining. It was nasty," he said. "And they didn't even think twice." Cort also says the Flight for Life pilot took a risk by flying in the bad weather to land in a tricky spot to rescue him. Cort was flown out of the area that night.

He's been recovering at St. Anthony Hospital since then. It's likely he'll be released from the hospital this week, but it will be several months before he's able to climb again. "I'll probably be out of climbing for about a year," he said. "But I'm talking to you." (Source: From a posting on mountainproject.com, appears to be from an interview piece with a local television station)

Analysis

Yes, he descended the route as did Lamb on his first reconnoiter of the east face. It is interesting that the first time anyone climbed on the east face, it was The Reverend Lamb during his recon, on descent. He peered over at the east face from the top, decided that it looked feasible, and went down. On his way down this moderately angled snow ramp, he slipped and went all the way to the bottom. He wound up near Chasm Lake unscathed. This is how Lamb's Slide got its name. The guy who slipped last weekend was merely descending in the time-honored tradition.

I'm glad he is ok. I saw the blurb on the news. His wife's comments were rather interesting. She thought it was cool and exciting. My wife would have killed me. (Source: Tom Hansen, posted on mountainproject.com)

Further analysis by RMNP Park Ranger Ryan Schuster:

Lamb's Slide has been the scene of numerous accidents during its storied history. It is a high profile couloir on a high profile mountain and it receives a lot of attention. Starting in late April and lasting until October, people come in droves to ski, climb, descend and traverse this couloir. The couloir itself goes through many "stages" during this time and the conditions encountered are HIGHLY variable. This accident happened in late August, a time when Lamb's Slide is beginning to enter its last "stage" before winter. This last stage is characterized by a lack of seasonal snowfall cover and an abundance of black alpine ice.

According to the victim's partners, the three climbers intended to climb the Kiener's Route on Longs Peak. None of the men had climbed the route before and they had limited experience climbing on routes such as this. They had a rope with them, but stated that they had made a decision not to use it because of the amount of rock that was falling down the couloir. They said that they felt that they could move faster unroped, thus exposing themselves to the rockfall hazard for a shorter period of time. All three men were wearing helmets and crampons and had mountaineering ice axes.

The decision whether or not to rope up for this portion of the climb is worthy of some discussion. These men were well equipped for the climb, having brought all of the standard safety equipment available to them for this type of excursion. However, when they made the decision to coil up the rope and climb the couloir without employing belays, they were following an old adage in mountaineering that speed is safety. That decision was a calculated risk based on their belief that the falling rock hazard was a greater relative risk than an unroped fall down the couloir.

While this concept of moving with speed in the high country is a valid one, it needs to be taken into context amongst several factors. How experienced are the climbers? How familiar with the route, environment, and style of climbing is the group? How difficult is the climbing? What is the hazard that is making us want to move faster? Can the hazard be avoided or mitigated? Do we need to compromise our safety to move faster? What are the consequences if we are compromising safety?

A constant reassessment of your situation and the hazards present is a vital part of maximizing safety in the high country. Answering questions like the ones listed above can help refine your calculated risk taking skills. In this incident I believe a self-examination and questioning session of the situation may have revealed that the hazard (rockfall) was caused by rapidly warming temperatures associated with the time of year. A possible mitigation of the hazard could include a much earlier start or waiting for a hard, overnight freeze. Perhaps the conditions were so warm that the hazard was ever-present. If this was the case, maybe the climb should not have been attempted, because the unroped climbing risk was too great given climber experience and ability level.

These are difficult decisions to make when confronted with them under stressful circumstances. The best way to make the correct decision is to constantly reevaluate your situation and talk it out with your partners. Ask yourselves, "What is going to get me hurt?" These men made the best decision they could at the time and I can find no fault in their decision to climb unroped.

FALL ON ROCK, OFF ROUTE, FAILURE TO TURN BACK, PARTY SEPARATED, INEXPERIENCE, INADEQUATE EQUIPMENT
Idaho, Lost River Range, Mount Church

On August 4, I.C. (41) and B.B. (36) set out to climb the standard route on Mount Church (12,200 feet) in the Lost River Range.

The approach to Mount Church begins with a strenuous 1.5 miles, one thousand foot climb through the forested bottom of the Jones Creek Canyon. The route then climbs a side canyon for fourteen hundred feet to a ridge which divides Jones Creek from an unnamed drainage to the west. The bottom is blocked repeatedly by the meandering Jones Creek, which zigzags back and forth leaving steeply cut banks, covered with tangled brush and downed timber. The approach route is so difficult that it takes most climbing groups more than two hours to reach the point where the route leaves the canyon bottom. On the day of the accident, there were no other climbers on the route.

About half way through the Jones Creek bottom, the climbers left the route and started to climb a steep side canyon. It appears that at first they believed they already crossed the entire Jones Creek section of the approach and were on the route. After climbing roughly 800 feet, they realized their mistake and attempted to regain the route by climbing north through a large Class 5 cliff band. I.C. was climbing above B.B. and moving over a rock wall that took her out of his view. I.C. told B.B. "Don't climb that. That was stupid." She directed him to climb back to the base of the cliffs while she looked for a route down the other side of the obstacle she just climbed.

B.B. started down but got stuck on a ledge. As he was looking for a route he heard I.C. call his name. Moments later, he heard rocks falling from I.C's direction. He also spotted contents from her pack falling down the face and then saw her falling, ricocheting off a ledge, and then continuing to fall out of his view.

At 11:12 a.m., B.B. called 911 on his cell phone, reported the accident and advised he was stuck on a ledge. Custer/Butte County SAR team and Portneuf Life Flight responded to the scene. Shortly after 12:00 p.m., as the rescue team was approaching the mouth of Jones Creek, the rescuers witnessed a violent thunder storm and saw several bolts of lightning strike the upper slopes of Mount Church and nearby Donaldson Peak. The upper part of the route was covered with a layer of hail. Most of the lightning strikes were above the accident scene. After reaching the scene, the rescuers confirmed I.C. had died in the fall. Her injuries consisted of a broken neck and severe head injuries. The rescue team performed a roped rescue for B.B and then walked him out to his truck.

About 2:00 p.m., during the rescue of B.B, the team experienced another series of less intense thunderstorms. During the rescue and subsequent investigation, rockfall was a continual hazard facing the rescuers. Rain from that system produced slippery conditions in the canyon that ultimately caused two rescuers to slip and sustain injuries as they hauled out I.C.'s body.

Analysis

Mount Church is one of nine 12,000-foot summits in Idaho. In recent years, climbing all of these peaks has become a popular pursuit for Idaho climbers. The Lost River Range is rugged, steep, and wild. Other than Mount Borah, Idaho's highest summit, the summits in the range are approached cross country through difficult, debris-filled, cliff-lined canyons.

The climbers had a topo map and route description from a hiking guidebook. I.C. was a novice climber who had started sport climbing in the spring of 2006. Two weeks prior to the accident, she successfully climbed the busy standard route (mostly trail) on Mount Borah. Her partner was an avid hiker but did not have any climbing experience.

This accident occurred due to a combination of the inexperience of both climbers and the difficulty of the terrain. Mount Church is not a peak which can be safely climbed by inexperienced climbers. Jones Creek is extremely wild and unforgiving and the bottom of Jones Creek constantly changes from year to year. Ascending the canyon requires physical conditioning, endurance, prior off-trail hiking experience, mental toughness and map reading skills.

The canyon walls are steep and crowned by broken cliffs. Experienced climbers who would have known from reviewing the topographic map and scouting the route from the valley floor that there were no non-technical routes up the west side of the canyon. Despite the technical nature of the canyon walls, the climbers left the canyon at the 8,200-foot contour and climbed up the wall to roughly 8,900 feet. As they ascended the slope, they crossed steep, cliffy terrain and a face that steepened as they continued their ascent. The unsuitability of the canyon wall for inexperienced, unequipped climbers is highlighted by the fact that when I.C. fell, she dropped more than 150 feet, bounced off at least three wide ledges, landed on a talus slope, and then rolled to a stop some 80 feet below the bottom of the cliff.

Inexperience also played into the decision to leave the route. Although B.B was unsure of why they prematurely left Jones Creek, it was likely, due to the difficulty of the terrain, that they believed they had actually reached the correct turning point. In reality they had traveled less than a mile–underestimating the time it takes to cross such inhospitable country. It is also possible B.B. and I.C. left the route, in an attempt to avoid the strain of climbing through the obstacles littering the Jones Creek bottom.

Inexperience was also demonstrated by their decision to continue onto technical terrain without adequate climbing equipment. While technical climbing equipment was not necessary for the standard route, the climbers did not recognize the need for such equipment when they ventured out onto the cliff band.

The climbers got off to a late (8:00 a.m.) departure on a day when the weather forecast called for thundershowers. The early development of thundershowers made the climb unwise, as the majority of the route crosses exposed ridges and faces. B.B did not mention that weather concerns factored into their decisions.

Finally, their decision making process was simply to react to obstacles by changing directions. They had several opportunities to retreat but did not consider this option until they were in serious trouble. (Source: Edited from a report by Wes Collins, Butte County Sheriff, Tom Lopez, and Perineum Life Flight RN Lance Taysom)

FALL ON ROCK, NO HELMET
Maine, Acadia National Park, Gunklandia

On October 8th around 11:30 a.m., my girlfriend, a group of friends, and I were top-roping Old Town and a few adjacent routes at the Precipice. Two young women were climbing the nearby route Gunklandia. For reasons unknown, the experienced lead climber, L.B. (21), lowered off after climbing through the crux and switched ends with her partner S.B. (21), a beginner. Minutes later I looked up to see S.B. falling. Her feet hit a small ledge and sent her over backwards, and as the rope came tight, she hit the back of her head on the wall. The fall was estimated to be 30 feet. After righting herself, she felt the back of her head, which was covered in blood. Her partner lowered her. My girlfriend called 911 on her cell phone and I came over to assist. S.B. had a deep gouge on the back of her head that was bleeding profusely. Using a t-shirt and athletic tape, we bandaged her head, and after L.B. (EMT) looked for spinal injury, we assisted her in walking her down the trail to meet the park rangers.

After the rangers took over her care, I went up Old Town and rapped down Gunklandia to retrieve their gear. Her last piece, a #4 BD stopper, was clipped to the rope with a long sling. There were three other pieces of gear, all stoppers clipped to the rope. No gear failed and all the placements looked secure. It is not known if S.B. placed any of the gear, since they had switched rope ends. The area she fell from was past the difficulties, and she reported "just slipping". There were ample places for protection in the area she fell.

Analysis

It is fairly certain a helmet in this fall could have significantly reduced the seriousness of the injury. One can speculate about inexperience, inadequate protection, climbing above one's limit, etc. What one can not speculate on is whether a helmet would have reduced this injury. Of the dozen or so climbers in the area that day, only a minority wore helmets. This occurred three days after an earthquake had released tons of rock in this area. (Source: David Lottmann, EMS Climbing Guide)

RAPPEL ERROR—INCORRECT SET UP AT ANCHOR, HASTE, FAILURE TO CHECK SYSTEM, DEVIATION FROM ROUTINE, DISTRACTION
North Carolina, Table Rock Mountain, The North Ridge

Around 2:30 p.m. on May 27th, Donald Gallo (39), Somsanouck Gallo (40), along with a friend, M. E., set out to climb The North Ridge, a 5.5 trad route on Table Rock. The three had arrived the night before and this was the first route of the holiday weekend. The area was busy, since much of the mountain was closed to climbing during the falcons' nesting season. A second group, with two adults, P.M., E.W., and three children, had earlier set up a top-rope, anchored at the end of The North Ridge's first pitch, about 130 feet into the climb. A third group arrived, C.T. & K.T., and after speaking to M.E., they decided to climb a nearby route, White Lightning. This third group reported a sense of frustration about how long the second group had been top-roping this trad route.

The decision was made that Donnie, Som, and M.E. could safely lead The North Ridge, while the top-roping continued. Donnie led the first pitch. He then belayed Som up to the ledge. Before M. E. cleaned the route, a man from the second group, P. M., climbed to the anchors on his top-rope. M.E. then cleaned the route. There were now four people on the ledge.

It was somewhat cooler and windy on the ledge compared to the base. Som was cold and wanted to get down to get her jacket and warm up. The fixed anchors on the ledge consisted of three pitons with static line, equalized to a master point. Concern was raised as to the safety of rapping down on just these points. P.M. offered to let Donnie, Som, and M. E. rappel off of his top-rope anchor, which was already set up. Everyone agreed. Donnie backed up the three pitons with a cam. While Donnie and P.M. were setting up the rappel off of the pitons, Som and M.E., along with P.M. whose anchor it was, were preparing the rappel from the top-rope anchor. While all of this was happening, the leader from the third group, K.T., had arrived at the ledge and was bringing up his second, C.T. Several people on the ledge mentioned later that there was a lot of talking, "chatting about whatever." It was very distracting, but no one said anything about it at the time.

What exactly happened next is in dispute. We know that the two ropes were tied together in order to make the long rappel to the ground. Either M.E. handed the ropes, already tied, to P.M. who placed them in the carabiners, or P.M. passed one rope through the carabiners to M.E. who removed the rope from the carabiner, tied them together, and then placed them in the carabiners. Either way, the ropes were placed into the carabiners. Donnie tossed the ropes over the edge. They caught on a ledge below. Usually Donnie would have pulled them up and tossed them again, but he figured Som could just toss them over when she got there.

Som put the ropes through her ATC and attached them to her harness with a locking carabiner. She asked that another locking carabiner be placed into the master point. (There was an unused locker hanging nearby). It was placed into the system, next to the other carabiners. Donnie now believes that Som thought there was something not right about the anchor, but wasn't sure what it was. While she was an experienced climber, she relied on help from more experienced climbers to set-up the ropes and to double-check her.

M.E. checked the carabiners and made sure they were locked. M.E. offered Som an autoblock, but she declined, saying she never used one. Som unclipped her safety line. M.E. stopped her and had her re-clip and test the set-up before rappelling. She re-clipped and weighted the ropes. Everything seemed fine. She unclipped her safety line and began her rappel.

Som descended, first walking backwards and feeding out rope down a long slab. She then bounced on the ropes trying to feed them through the ATC. When she got to the end of the first slab and weighted the rope fully, there was a "pop" sound. Som went over backwards, hit her back on the slab below, slid down the slab and over the edge. The entire rope followed her.

In the chaos that followed, great attempts were made by climbers on the ledge to keep everyone safe and get them down as quickly as possible. Donnie descended first, followed by M.E., P.M., C.T., and after pulling the last of the gear, K.T. descended on the three pitons.

E.W. was on the ground with his kids when the accident occurred. He ran over to Som and held her. She was not breathing and had no pulse. When Donnie arrived, he began CPR, but to no avail. Climbers at the bottom called 911, and nearby Boy Scouts ran to the parking area to meet them. Checks of Som's equipment revealed no problems. Her harness, rappel device, and ropes were all connected correctly. She was wearing a helmet.

Analysis

The rappel rope was set up incorrectly and the mistake was not caught when checking the system prior to rappel. After the two ropes were tied together using an overhand knot with 18-inch tail, they were improperly placed in the anchor system. We believe that both ropes were placed in the carabiners together with the knot and tail on one side of the anchor carabiners and both ropes coming out of the other side. The ropes were therefore never actually connected to the anchor system. Som was very cold and anxious to get down. This was clearly a factor in her ability to properly assess the system set-up.

When the system was checked, the locking carabiners were pinched and then locked. Som weighted the system and it held her. Now if the carabiners are locked and when weighting the rope it holds you, you would think all is well and proceed on rappel. However, Som was standing on a slab and weighed only about 85 pounds. Therefore, only a small amount of weight was actually placed on the system during this crucial check. The checks that were completed were typical checks on a system prior to rappel. Som proceeded on rappel and when her full weight came on the system at the edge of the slab, the knot pulled through the carabiners and released the ropes she was rappelling on.

There were four people involved in the rappel set-up. All were experienced climbers, including Som. There was no single person in charge or second person responsible for checking the work of the first. M.E. thought she was just checking P.M.'s set up since he was there before her, and it was his top-rope anchor. P.M. thought M.E. was setting everything up the way she wanted and didn't have the chance to check the system before Som began her rappel. Donnie didn't feel right about the whole anchor situation, but didn't say anything about. He focused his attention to backing up the pitons and setting up the second rappel. There were two climbers between him and Som. The activity level on the ledge was high. There was a lot of talking about the gear as well as general chatting. This was very distracting and most of the climbers on the ledge believe this to be a very important factor contributing to the accident.

In addition, the safety routine established by Donnie and Som, which was *always* followed, was not followed on this day. As a rule, a heavier climber always went first and Som rappelled after in case she needed assistance. She went first on this day. As a rule, Donnie *always* set up the rappel and double-checked the system before anyone went anywhere. On this day, other experienced climbers took that responsibility.

The error made when setting up the ropes was missed when checking the system. A critical visual inspection of the rope attachment should have revealed the misplaced lines. The long tail most likely contributed to the confusion, as it appeared to be set up correctly. In addition, a physical trace test was not performed. Physically touching and tracing the rope through the closed system would allow the climber to notice any part of the rope placement that was not where they wanted it. (Checking the anchor and harness can be done using a similar tracing method.)

Remember that everyone involved was an experienced climber. Mistakes can happen to anyone. Be careful. Check and double check each other thoroughly and retrace the system. Don't rush. Limit distractions. Take care when altering your set routine. (Source: Jill Machniak-Gallagher)

FALL ON ROCK, NO HARD HAT
New Hampshire, Cathedral Ledge, Turner's Flake

This afternoon (August 6) while I was belaying my girlfriend on the first pitch of Thin Air, I witnessed Doug M. (50+) take a leader fall on Turners Flake. It is estimated he fell 30–40 feet. He immediately stated he had broken his wrist (later confirmed it was broken in three places) and was lowered to the ground by his belayer. A friend of mine took over the belay of my girlfriend while a nearby climber and I headed down to offer assistance. Doug M. was completely alert, but had some bruising and blood on his head (no helmet). Because of this, I offered to call for an ambulance, which he accepted. His belayer slung his arm and we walked him out to the road. After meeting the ambulance, I headed back up to retrieve his gear. His last piece was a small cam placed in a pocket to the right of the flake. This piece failed and hit him in the forehead causing it to bleed. (No stitches were needed.) The next piece, about ten feet down, was a #3 Camalot, placed before the flake widens and becomes a little run out. His was climbing on double 8.6-mm Beal ropes that had been used for two ice seasons and two rock seasons and had not taken any leader falls. The belayer was anchored and stated he was lifted off the ground and had loaded the anchor.

Analysis

Of note is an accident that occurred last year under almost the exact same circumstances on this route, on which it is difficult to reduce rope drag with or without using doubles. The victim last year was on doubles, fighting with drag. He fell, flipped upside down, and suffered injuries to his head and face. He was not wearing a helmet. I assume that the additional stretch of skinnier ropes in this situation (especially if they were twins used improperly) may have led to a longer fall. It appeared that as the fall was being arrested, Doug hit a small ledge/flake about 30 feet up the climb, one of the only protrusions it is possible to hit.

It is hard to understand why people would climb this route without a helmet, as falling upside down is a very real possibility. Ironically, while hiking back up to retrieve the gear, a party on Standard Route dislodged significant rock-fall that impacted the descent trails from Turners Flake. (Source: Dave Lottmann, EMS Climbing Guide)

(Editor's Note: In late November, Doug M. was involved in another serious accident, this time in Tuckerman Ravine. He was solo climbing near the center of the bowl, and on descent, he lost control of a glissade on ice. He was wearing crampons, so it became a tumbling fall that resulted in serious fractures. The weather turned extremely cold. Had he not been rescued, it is likely he would have perished.)

FALLING ROCK—FOOTHOLD CAME OFF
New Hampshire, Cannon Cliff, Moby Grape

On September 2, my climbing partner Jon Sykes and I had gotten an alpine start to climb on Cannon Cliff hoping to beat the weather coming in with hurricane Ernesto. I was aid-climbing up the first pitch of One Drop of Water and was only 15 feet from the ledge I hoped to use as a belay when I heard that sound every Cannon climber fears: rockfall. I immediately looked to my right and saw a large pile of rock dislodge from low on the cliff and a climber's rope come tight. Jon and I started yelling to see if they were OK and got the reply we expected, "Help!!" I abandoned my climb and got down as quickly as possible, but setting a good anchor and rappelling seems to take a very long time when there is an emergency. I finally reached the ground and joined Jon and the other climbers.

Mike had been leading the original first pitch of Moby Grape. He had climbed up about 30 feet and got his first piece of gear, a large cam, in a good crack. He then climbed another 15 feet and was standing on a large piece of rock when it gave way under his weight. The largest chunk was under him, but there were other smaller rocks bouncing around. His gear held him as he fell onto it, but it seems one of the fragments of rock hit his leg, leaving a large gash close to the bone on his lower left leg. The largest piece, surfboard shaped, about the size of a sofa and one-and-a-half-feet thick, came straight down and lodged itself between two boulders. The rest of the fragments showered off to the left avoiding the direct path to the belayer.

The rescue that followed is the reason I write this story. I was impressed at how quickly and how well all the climbers on the cliff that day came together and evacuated one of our own. In addition to Jon and me, Mike's partners (his brothers Chris and Mark), Art, a local guide with two clients, and six others were present. The litter was promptly retrieved from its cache at the base of Whitney Gilman. Mike was already bandaged up and lifted himself into the litter. He seemed in good spirits despite his situation and was very alert and oriented. We carried him along the base of the cliff to the top of the climber's trail. The rest of the way down was over the talus slope, a large maze of boulders with very dangerous footing and many unstable rocks. We chose not to walk through this but to pass the litter along hand over hand. This means when you hand off the head you need to get to the feet as soon as possible. With only 13 people, this was difficult. By the time two Fish and Game Officers and three Pemi Valley Rescuers arrived on scene, we were in the wooded section below the talus slope and had completed more than three- quarters of the carry out. With their help, we reached the Fish and Game vehicle on the bike path and loaded Mike into the back.

The total time from the accident until we reached the bike path was less than two hours. We made very good time considering the terrain. This was in part to several factors. First, Mike and his partners were incredibly lucky that there were not more injuries. Second, there is a litter available at the base of the Whitney Gilman ridge. And finally, there were enough competent and willing people on the cliff that day.

Although one would hope that every one would volunteer to help a fellow climber, the presence of people with rescue experience was important. My final note is that local rescue teams are a great asset and a very important part of search and rescue but nothing beats a self-evacuation with on-scene resources.

Analysis

I want to make it known that Mike is a very good climber and experienced on Cannon. This is an accident that could happen to anyone, regardless of experience.

Cannon is a very serious place and not a cliff to be under estimated. Mike and his partners were very lucky that much worse did not happen. Rock-fall is very common and a human presence makes it even more likely. When climbing on existing routes, variations or new routes, it is important to be aware of the rock. Always tap blocks to see if they move or sound hollow and avoid ones that do. Be wary of detached flakes and rubble piles.

I know this sounds obvious, but I feel many climbers come from Conway's solid rock and are not as used to this terrain. Don't think because Whitney/Gilman or Moby Grape are popular that they don't have loose rock. Both have signs of recent rock-fall. Everyone knows the Old Man came down recently and Whaleback Crack not too much earlier. It is only a matter of time before the Sickle and the Fickle Finger go too. The talus slope is also active and not a place to be wearing sandals, as one rescuer was. (We did request he not carry and gave him other tasks to perform.) So please, one climber to another, respect [this] cliff and climb safely. (Source: Peet Danen)

(Editor's Note: On Mount Washington, one of New Hampshire's favorite winter climbing arenas, there were six significant accidents. Four of them were the result of glissading with crampons on. One involved a solo ice climber who fell 40 feet and sustained multiple arm fractures. The final one was in Central Gully of Huntington Ravine, where five climbers were practicing skills when an avalanche struck them, resulting in one broken leg. On this particular day, December 30, there were strong indicators of increasing avalanche danger because of fresh snow and high winds. Additionally, they were not equipped with beacons, probes, or shovels.)

VARIOUS FALLS ON ROCK, INADEQUATE BELAYS, AND INADEQUATE PROTECTION
New York, Mohonk Preserve, Shawangunks

We received twelve reports from this climbing area for the year 2006.

Of the nine falling accidents, eight occurred while leading and three involved protection pulling out. There were three inadequate belaying situations. In one case, the belayer dropped the climber to the ground.

The average age of those involved was 35 and the average difficulty of the climbs on which the incidents occurred was 5.6. The level of experience of five of those involved is unknown. All but one of the rest were experienced. (Source: From reports submitted by Mohonk Preserve)

FALL ON SNOW—SKI MOUNTAINEERING, INADEQUATE EQUPMENT FOR THE CONDITIONS
Oregon, Mount Hood, Reid Glacier

On May 6, four experienced climbers were circumnavigating Mount Hood (crossing Yokum Ridge) at the 7,600-foot elevation when telemark skier Jeremy (41) lost his edge on an icy patch and fell about 300 feet over rocky slabs. The other three skiers (randonée) were able locate the subject from a rockfall area and make cellphone contact to initiate a rescue. Portland Mountain Rescue teams performed an extensive ground evacuation using multiple raising systems to an awaiting ski area snowcat.

The fall resulted in multiple fractures.

Analysis

Jeremy was using telemark equipment whilst his companions were randonée equipped. If the first skier across the icy slope had warned of conditions, perhaps Jeremy could have shifted to crampons. It is not known if the skiers were using self-arresting ski poles. (Source: Jeff Scheetz, Portland Mountain Rescue)

FALL ON SNOW/ICE—UNABLE TO SELF-ARREST, INADEQUATE PROTECTION
Oregon, Mount Hood, South Side

On June 17, Aaron Dunlap (31), Jeremy Hawkins (32), and Brad Wood (30), were just below the Pearly Gates when two of them lost their footing and slid down the 50-degree slope, stopping about 450 feet below in the Devil's Kitchen area about the 11,000-foot level.

The impact during the fall caused serious injuries (fractures, abrasions, lacerations) to Dunlop and Hawkins. One climbing helmet was broken during the fall. Wood was able to walk off the mountain.

Analysis

The icy conditions caused the climbers to place protection, but the force of the fall ripped out the piece. Roped teams must be proficient at self-arrest, and group arrest. (Source: Jeff Scheetz, Portland Mountain Rescue, and an article from *The Seattle Times* on June 18)

FALL ON ROCK, CLIMBING ROPE UNDER LEG, FATIGUE
Oregon, Smith Rock State Park, Five Gallon Buckets

On October 29, Matt Amling (21) of Portland traveled to Smith Rock State Park with his climbing class from a Willamette Valley Community College. The class was working on Five Gallon Buckets, a 5.8 climb rated four stars by Jonathan Thesenga in his new guide *Smith Rock Select*, published in 2006 by Wolverine Publishing, Newcastle, CO.

Matt was lead-climbing his final pitch of the day. He notes that he was pretty tired and was just about to clip the top anchors when his instructor warned him that his climbing rope was under his leg. At that moment, Matt lost friction with the crag and fell. He dropped about ten feet, ending up jerked upside down. His head banged hard against the rock, he recalls. He was not knocked unconscious, but he received a cut on his forehead, perhaps from his helmet, that later required stitches. He was bleeding profusely.

The instructor called 911 from a cellphone. Matt was lowered to the ground and was helped down the climber's trace to a waiting State Park ATV which transported him up the steep trail to waiting Paramedics from Redmond Fire Department.

The Paramedics cleaned the cut and applied a temporary bandage and agreed that he could be transported by the Instructor in a private car to the ER, thereby saving the high cost of ambulance service. He was stitched up at the ER and released.

Analysis

Five Gallon Buckets is completely bolted and is a very popular Smith Rock top rope climb. If one allows the rope to pass under a leg and then falls, he or she may be jerked upside-down at the end of the fall. Keep the climbing rope in front of your legs. If Matt had not been wearing a climbing helmet, he feels he might have died.

This mishap is one of five reported minor accidents to sport climbers at Smith Rock in 2006. There were several un-reported accidents that were resolved unofficially by the injured climbers and their friends. (Source: Robert Speik)

STRANDED, LATE START, WEATHER, EXPOSURE, PROBABLE FALL ON SNOW/ICE (TWO), AND HYPOTHERMIA (ONE)
Oregon, Mount Hood, Cooper Spur

This high profile accident used such technological search tools as airborne thermal imaging, unmanned drones, and cellphone localization. It received national media coverage for more than a week. The writer has attempted to limit conclusions on facts and observations obtained through interviews and correspondence with on-scene rescuers. However, until more clues are uncovered with the melting snowpack, some uncertainty remains. Presented here are the most probable scenarios consistent with all known facts.

On December 6, three highly experienced climbers, Kelly James (48), Brian Hall (37), and Jerry Cooke (36), drove to the Cooper Spur winter trailhead and hiked the ski trail to the warming hut at Tilly Jane Campground.

Other visitors at the hut described the group as well equipped for their climb (stove, fuel, bivy gear, shovel, etc). On the way from Hood River, they left a note at a USFS ranger station with their plans to climb the North Face Gully and descend the route. On December 7, the party probably ascended the lower Cooper Spur route, thereby accessing the Eliot Glacier. It is likely that they bivouacked on the glacier before reaching the bergschrund start of their North Face route. On December 8, the group summited late in the day. From the summit, faint tracks led down the upper portion of the Wy'east route (ridge above Steel Cliff) several hundred yards before turning east down the fall line. About 500 feet below the crest, the party constructed a three-person snow cave, providing shelter and rest while waiting for better visibility before continuing their descent the next day. After traveling approximately 300 yards from the snow cave, the party reached the upper couloir of the Cooper Spur route. The North Face Couloir route merges here also. At this point, they may have recognized their previous climb and thus the starting point for the descent of the Cooper Spur route.

At this exposed 50-degree slope, they placed a snow anchor (two pickets and webbing) and dug a belay/rappel platform adjacent to a rock outcropping. It appears that a falling accident involved two climbers (Hall and Cooke). The searchers found two ice tools, two short pieces of 7.5 mm climbing rope (about 40 feet), a single glove, and a foam pad on the belay platform.

On December 10, the party failed to meet friends waiting at Timberline Lodge and the Hood River County Sheriff was notified. At 3:45 p.m., Kelly James placed a four-minute cell phone call to his wife in Texas indicating that he was in a snow cave near the summit while his two companions were descending the mountain to seek assistance. The call ended abruptly, causing concern. Sensing distress, James' wife called authorities to report the incident. The content of the call was described as "disorganized" and was "not good information" according to a sheriff's deputy. Eight days later, James was found deceased, lightly clothed in the large snow cave with minimal equipment (no sleeping bag, no bivy sack, no insulating pad, no stove). The cave did contain his backpack, cellphone, ice tool, crampons, harness, and belay/rappel device. A subsequent medical examiner report stated that he died of hypothermia, but no other injuries were discovered. The other two climbers were not found and are presumed dead.

Analysis

Photographs retrieved from a camera found in the snow cave suggest that the party was on the face late in the day due to a slow start. The pictures also indicate that the party was traveling light, suggesting an equipment cache below the start of the climb. The absence of a summit photo also suggests summit arrival after dark. From footprints found on the summit area, it appears that the party could not find the start of the Southside descent route (rimmed rock formations known as the "Pearly Gates") due to poor visibility (snow spindrift or ground /fog) or the loss of daylight. They ended up descending the upper Wy'east route.

After several hundred yards, the group decided to descend the Cooper Spur route instead. This decision was likely prompted by the milder winds experienced on the easterly (leeward) exposure. After leaving the windy crest, they dug a large snow cave, seeking shelter and awaiting a break in the storm. Faint tracks suggest that at least one climber explored the area below the cave (top of Black Spider Couloir system) probably looking for a safe descent route. Winds did not drop significantly until about 5:00 p.m., so it is likely they remained in the cave until Sunday morning. They probably left the cave about 7:00 a.m. Sunday to continue their traverse/descent via the Cooper Spur route. At the anchor site, the two pieces of cut rope, ice tools, one glove, and steep terrain all suggest a catastrophic falling accident. A small avalanche could also produce the same effect.

The initial scenario carried by the media involves the intentional separation of the party at the snow cave. James, presumably in a weaker state, was left behind while Hall and Cooke descended to get assistance. This corresponds with the message James gave his wife. However, it is difficult to explain why a 911 call was not placed, since there were at least two phones in the party.

Leaving a fellow climber behind is a desperate action, and the obvious admission that a self-rescue was not possible. The snow cave was later shown to be cellphone friendly, at least for James' phone. Another inconsistency is the foam pad found at the belay/rappel anchor site. It seems unlikely that both Hall and Cooke would intentionally leave James lying on a snow cave floor without the very important insulating pad. The absence of any physical injury of James also does not support the "injured climber left behind" assumption, although he could have been suffering more than the others from exhaustion, hypothermia, or altitude sickness.

A different scenario which may better fit the facts supposes that the entire party left the snowcave seeking the Cooper Spur descent. At this point, the climbers may have optimistically expected self-rescue, so no 911 call was placed. A belaying or rappelling accident, avalanche, or perhaps an unroped fall by Cooke and Hall could have left James stranded at the belay/rappel anchor.

High winds, hard ice surface conditions, or unstable snow may have caused such an accident. As the sole survivor, James would be emotionally distraught, perhaps irrational, and may have forgotten his insulating pad as he returned to the snow cave.

The weather experienced by the party was predicted. During the approach, the party enjoyed fair weather. While on the North Face on Friday the climbers experienced cold temperatures (as low as 15 degrees F) and no solar heating for the entire ascent. Winds were estimated at 10–20 mph. Very early Saturday morning brought colder temperatures, several inches of snow, and higher winds.

Later in the day, summit wind estimates picked up to 35 mph sustained. On Sunday morning, the temperatures increased to about 20 degree F and the winds abated to about 20 mph. However, the arrival of a second storm front in the afternoon raised summit winds to about 45 mph sustained. Since the arrival of the first storm on Friday night, it is likely that the summit was engulfed in ground fog with very limited visibility. On late Sunday a severe storm system hit the mountain preventing searchers from approaching the summit for a full week.

The route conditions during this climb are believed to have been good. Aerial photographs taken one week later (after the major storm) suggest that there was adequate consolidated snow cover and sustained sub-freezing temperatures needed to cement the volcanic rock and provide purchase for crampon points and ice tools.

It is not known why the party started the climb so late in the morning, as they allowed themselves one-and-a-half days for the approach from the trailhead. Retreating from this route would be difficult and would involve many roped pitches of down-climbing or rappelling, which is slow even for a party of two. Once on the route, proceeding to the summit was likely viewed as the fastest way off the route. The fault in this logic is that getting off the mountain can be much harder than completing the ascent route.

While experienced climbers are capable of surviving weeks in snow caves if they have appropriate equipment (extra food, stoves, bivouac gear), such equipment may slow the speed of approach ascent and retreat. This may cause an increase in overall risk to the climbers when timing or a time limitations are necessary to safely complete a climb. Winter climbing conditions can be particularly difficult due to the short days, low temperatures, frequent and long duration storms. For this particular accident, it appears that all of the bivy gear was cached below the technical route and did not contribute to the survivability of the party. "Travel light" practitioners assume the risk associated with delaying action of injuries or storms. It appears that James was only able to survive in the snow cave for three to four days with his minimal equipment.

Climbers carrying cellphones are not always capable of reporting distress situations, especially in wilderness environments lacking urban cell coverage. In this case, the cellphone message appeared to be too late and non-specific to be useful. Also, radio-location of cellphone signals was not precise enough to be helpful. For those climbers who feel the need to rely on high technology, a Personal Locating Beacon (PLB) will provide fast and accurate location information to relevant authorities. Alternatively, a GPS-assisted cellphone (called Enhanced E911) could also help in situations where only a single cell tower is accessible.

As a direct consequence of this high profile search, the Oregon state legislature proposed bills which mandate electronic signaling devices (Personal Locator Beacons, Mountain Locator Beacon, GPS receiver with cellphone, and/or two-way radios) for all climbs above 10,000 on Mount Hood. Most local rescue personal and climbers encourage the use of such equipment but do not believe its use should be required. For this particular accident, the stormy weather delayed reaching even known locations in the summit area, so electronic signaling would not likely have affected the outcome. (Source: Jeff Scheetz, Portland Mountain Rescue)

(Editor's Note: Robert Speik, one of our sources for reports from Oregon, has an interesting website readers may wish to access. It is as follows: http://www.traditionalmountaineering.org)

FALL ON SNOW, CLIMBING UNROPED
Utah, Mount Olympus

On January 21, a group of seven climbers from the Korean Alpine Club of Utah started an ascent of Mount Olympus from the Pete's Rock trailhead. Their plan was to snowshoe to the South summit via the Tolcat Trail, then down-climb to the couloir between the two summits and descend the couloir back to the trail.

After summiting, the group began the down-climb to the couloir. This is a 50–70-degree snow climb, with areas of exposed rock and ice. The easiest route descends for about 300 feet and then traverses slightly West before continuing to the saddle between the summits. The climbers had removed their snowshoes and were down-climbing unroped and without crampons.

In Han (47) and Usun Park (63) descended first, missing the traverse and continuing lower in the fall line, where the slope angle gets steeper. Han was able to make it down safely, but Park slipped and tumbled 100-plus feet to the couloir, landing on the 35-degree snowfield below. Han yelled up to the others to try to traverse over and take the lower angle route down, but they traversed East instead of West, taking an equally steep line. During that descent, both Jakyung Sung (51) and Abeyta Kiok (50) slipped and fell all the way to the snowfield below, while Oknam Han (48), Inheu Yun (41), and Hoon Lee (51) were able to down-climb successfully.

Park was able to get a cellphone out of his pack and call a friend in town, who in turn called 911. Six members of Salt Lake County SAR were flown to the summit of Mount Olympus, with sleeping bags, food, stoves, medical supplies and rope rescue gear. They rappelled the route the climbers had intended to descend, fixing three pitches to the saddle and a fourth pitch down onto the snowfield. Arriving there, they found the climbers all together, with the three injured climbers having been helped into additional clothing.

After medical assessments, an additional flight was made to drop a bean bag vacuum splint at the saddle for Sung, who had a suspected pelvic fracture. Rescuers shoveled a large platform in the snow, packaged Sung in the vacuum splint and a sleeping bag, and prepared the other injured climbers as well as they could to spend the rest of the night on the mountain. Oknam Han would also spend the night, as she was unable to walk with frostbitten toes. The low temperature that night was six degrees F.

Three rescuers gathered the remaining functional snowshoes and started the hike out with In Han, Lee, and Yun at 3:00 a.m., arriving at the Neff's Canyon Trailhead around 7:00 a.m. During that time, the other rescuers repeatedly checked vital signs on the injured climbers, brewed hot water, and shoveled more snow. Shortly after sunrise, a Lifeflight helicopter began the first of seven hoist extractions for the four climbers and the three remaining rescuers, bringing the climbers to ambulances waiting at the trailhead.

Analysis

The group was experienced at this sort of winter mountaineering adventure, having summited peaks all around the Wasatch, but they seriously underestimated the difficulty of the down-climb off the summit of Mount Olympus. The route they descended became progressively steeper as they went. At any point before Park's initial fall, the group could have called a stop and returned the way they had come. After his fall, the urgency to aid an injured partner caused two more accidents. The group is incredibly fortunate to have had three major falls in a remote location on a cold night and still escape without any fatalities. (Source: Tom Moyer, Salt Lake Country Sheriff's Search and Rescue)

FALL ON ROCK, PROTECTION UNCLIPPED, INADEQUATE PROTECTION
Utah, Big Cottonwood Canyon, Beware of Dog

On July 2, Paul Sternman (24) suffered a ground-fall of approximately 60 feet on Beware of Dog, a 10d sport climb at the upper S-curves, Big Cottonwood Canyon. The route has four bolts. The first three cover the crux of the climb, followed by a long run-out on easier terrain. Paul was leading between the fourth bolt and the chains when he fell. This became a long fall because his quickdraw unclipped from the carabiner on the fourth bolt. His belayer tried to take in rope, but Paul hit the ground just as the rope started to become taut. He was wearing a helmet and the helmet did take a significant impact. SAR team members packaged him in a litter and vacuum splint, then lowered him one short pitch to gain clear distance from the wall where he was hoisted by a Lifeflight helicopter.

Analysis

The quickdraw was found on the ground with only one carabiner attached. The other carabiner, a Black Diamond straight gate, remained in place at the fourth bolt. Its gate had been forced open past the nose of the carabiner and was open as far as the gate hinge would allow. It had some new scarring on the surfaces facing away from the rock. The gate pin, hinge, and gate notch were all completely undamaged and the gate still moved freely.

The bolt had been placed in an extremely bad location. It was just above an edge on less than vertical rock, resulting in loading of the carabiner over the edge. In any orientation, the gate of this carabiner would have been in contact with the rock. This makes the gate vulnerable to being opened in a fall, which both reduces the strength of the carabiner and creates a possibility for unclipping to occur.

We believe that as Paul climbed above the bolt, rope drag lifted the quickdraw up so that it was positioned on the gate. When he fell, the gate was pushed open and pried sideways past the nose, allowing the quickdraw to release from the carabiner. It requires much less force to pry a gate sideways than it takes to break a carabiner.

Paul was described by his friends as being extremely safety conscious. Both his use of a helmet while leading a sport route and his other quickdraw placements on the route are consistent with this description. All of his draws were clipped correctly, and they were all set up identically, with a straight-gate carabiner clipped to the bolt and a wire gate carabiner clipped to the rope.

There are a few things that Paul could have done to reduce the chance of an accident. Some climbers carry one draw set up with locking carabiners for placements like this. In this case, a locking carabiner on the bolt-clipping end would probably have prevented the accident. There were also possible gear placements between the third and fourth bolts. An intermediate piece here would have prevented this from being a ground-fall. (Source: Tom Moyer, Salt Lake Country Sheriff's Search and Rescue)

FALL INTO CREVASSE
Washington, Mount Rainier, Ingraham Glacier

About 5:00 p.m. on July 7, rangers at Camp Muir were notified by Rainier Mountaineering, Inc., of a climbing team of three at the 13,000-foot level on the Ingraham Glacier in possible need of assistance. One of the team (49) was crossing a snow bridge when he fell ten feet into a crevasse. Though his fall was arrested by his two climbing partners, he injured his shoulder. They were descending slowly to their camp at Ingraham Flats.

Rangers Ken Davies and Lynn Finnel were dispatched from Camp Muir to assess and assist the injured climber. At Ingraham Flats, they found the team and Ken Davies, an EMT, performed an initial medical assessment. He placed a sling and swathe on the injured shoulder. The climber said he could walk, but that he could not tolerate any weight on his shoulder. The rangers assisted him in descending to Camp Muir. The climbers continued on down to the Paradise parking area. Enroute they met two physicians. Their examination indicated that the injury was probably a dislocation. (Source: *Bergtrage*)

(Editor's Note: This was the only report from Mount Rainier for the year. Note this data which comes from Ranger Mike Gauthier's website: www.mountrain-ierclimbing.blogspot.com

Total Climbers Registered in 2006 = 9,154, Independent Climbers = 5,022, Guides and Clients = 4,132, Total Summits = 5,787

"More exciting than summit attempts and success is the fact that we had no major rescues on the upper mountain in 2006! That's right, no fatalities or serious accidents above 10,000 feet. This is somewhat of a remarkable accomplishment, and the NPS would like to thank all the climbers for making safe decisions that contributed to this amazing statistic. No serious accidents: This is a trend we would like to see continue.")

FALL ON ROCK—DISLOCATED KNEE, FALL ON SNOW—UNABLE TO SELF-ARREST, EXCEEDING ABILITIES, INABILITY TO CONTINUE DUE TO INJURIES, TRYING TO PLEASE OTHERS, INADEQUATE COMMUNICATION
Washington, North Cascades, Mt. Baker, Spider/Formidable Couloir

Marty, Dave, Doug and I (Mike) all met as volunteers on a local mountain rescue team. Among the four of us we had varying degrees of rescue, mountaineering and rock climbing experience. Additionally, Dave and Doug are members of a popular mountaineering club. Doug is also a certified EMT.

On August 25th, we entered the North Cascades National Park to begin our journey along the popular Ptarmigan Traverse, a 25 mile, more or less, alpine traverse along the boundary of Skagit and Chelan Counties. The route spans from Cascade Pass southerly to Downey Creek. I'd completed this same traverse years ago with another friend from our rescue team.

On the morning of August 26th, we packed up camp, shouldered our 55-pound packs, left Kool-Aid Lake, and headed towards the Red Ledge, a narrow ledge cutting across the face of a reddish cliff band. Unfortunately, due to the late season snow conditions, the lower portion had to be gained by a short 4th-class climb. Doug brought up some concerns about climbing with his pack up this rock and suggested that we could do a pack haul, but a decision was made not to because we thought it would be fairly easy to carry them. (Doug later recalled that he'd felt like no one really seemed to listen to his suggestion, so he went with the flow.) Marty climbed first followed by Dave then Doug. I waited down below on the snow while Doug began to ascend a steep dirt bank to the base of the rock. I noticed he was having difficulty getting a good stance when he suddenly yelled and dropped to the ground. I quickly ascended and asked Marty and Dave to wait for a minute. When I got to Doug, he explained that he had weighted his foot at an odd angle causing his knee to dislocate. We pulled his pack off and talked about the situation. I told him we had three choices: rescue, hike out, or hike on. Doug thought that if we wrapped his knee, he could continue without incident. We taped him up with some athletic tape and hung there for a few minutes to see how it felt. Marty volunteered to descend and grab Doug's pack so Doug could climb without that extra weight. Doug climbed on without issue.

Later that day, from the top of the Middle Cascade Glacier we had to descend the Spider/Formidable Col. Again, due to the late season conditions, it was melted out about a third of the way down. After a short discussion with Doug, we decided that he would descend without his pack. I rigged a belay for Marty to descend with two packs. Dave started the descent first, followed by Doug, then Marty. After Marty got down to the top of the snow, he called, "Off belay," and I began my descent. Doug decided he could descend the snow with his pack, so he followed Dave while Marty waited for me. Once I made it down to the top of the snow with Marty, I started coiling the rope. That's when we heard Doug yell, "Falling!" Doug had fallen and self-arrested on the snow. I finished stowing the rope and Marty and I started to descend when we saw Doug fall again, but this time he didn't self-arrest. He remained on his butt and tried to control his slide. He couldn't control it and went feet first into a band of exposed rock separating the chute from the snowfield below. He flipped forward, skipping his helmet off the rocks and tumbled over until he hit the snow field and slid to a stop. Marty and I quickly descended. When we got down to Doug and Dave, Doug looked up and said, "I'm done." He had a laceration on the same knee he had dislocated earlier. This time there was deeper soft tissue damage and he couldn't bend his knee without a great deal of pain. He had some bumps and bruises and a good ding on his helmet that most likely would have resulted in a concussion had he not been wearing it.

I rigged a couple pickets and belayed Doug down the snow field with Marty and Dave assisting him to the boulders below. We found a large semi-flat rock and made it as comfortable as possible for Doug. We quickly resolved that two of us would head back to the Cascade Pass Trail head and initiate a rescue at first light while one stayed with Doug. I prepared dinner, Marty prepped the bivy site, and Dave climbed to the South Ridge of Formidable to see if he could get a signal on his cellular phone. Dave didn't make it back until after dark, but he had gotten out. The sheriff told him to expect to see a helicopter by 7:00 a.m. and to call him back if we hadn't seen it by 8:00 a.m. We spent that evening loading up Doug's pack with all of our nonessentials and extra food rations.

The next morning we placed a large red tarp on the snow field behind us, located a primary and secondary landing zone, had some breakfast, and waited for the helicopter.

An honorable mention should go out to Jake, a lone hiker who wandered the North Cascades taking pictures. He wandered into our bivy site to say hello and ask some route questions. We filled him in on our situation and he decided to hang around for some possible photo ops and offer his help if he could. (Thanks Jake!)

By about 7:50 a.m., we hadn't seen our helicopter yet, so Dave volunteered to once again climb the South Ridge of Formidable to contact the Sheriff. This was a commendable effort. Shortly after Dave's return to tell us they were enroute, we heard the buzzing of a helicopter from the south. We saw it fly in over Le Conte Mountain. They must have seen the couple camped down at Ying Yang lakes to our south because they decided to land there. It turned out to be the Chelan County Sheriffs Office. They took off again and made another attempt to locate us. We quickly grabbed our compasses and started flashing them with mirrors. It worked! They flew up to us and we quickly pointed out the two landing zones and after a few passes, they left. About 1:00 p.m., a second helicopter flew in from the north. They landed on our primary LZ without hesitation. After some assessment they maneuvered the bird to the secondary LZ, smaller and dangerously close to the snow slope behind us. Once they loaded Doug into the helicopter and took off, we shouldered our packs and headed back towards Cascade Pass.

Analysis

Though Marty, David, and I were comfortable climbing the 4th class rock up to the Red Ledge and descending the Spider/Formidable Couloir, Doug was not. His experience on rock was limited. There was a failure on our part for not communicating with Doug enough to recognize his level of comfort on that terrain. We failed to see the urgency when he suggested a pack-haul on the Red Ledge. This level of climbing continued intermittently and led Doug into having a raised level of anxiety throughout the day. There was a failure on Doug's part for not relaying his true level of discomfort to us adequately. It was a subtle communication breakdown which proved to be very dangerous in the end. It can be difficult to stay within your comfort zone in a changing environment. But it is extremely important to communicate effectively with your climbing partners to maintain safe climbing practices and stay within your comfort zone as an individual and as a team. Better communication on all of our part would have probably resulted in hauling our packs up the 4th class climb to gain the Red Ledge, changing route choices to better accommodate the team and rigging a belay down the Spider/Formidable Couloir. (Source: Edited slightly from a report submitted by Michael Nichols)

(Editor's Note: This was recorded in Table III as two incidents. There were several other incidents reported in Bergtrage this year, but without enough detail to enter them as narratives. They included a 65-foot fall into a crevasse on Mount Baker, resulting in a broken femur; a 60-foot leader fall in Leavenworth resulting in a fractured femur; a 60-foot fall on Little Si resulting in fractures; and a 30-foot fall on Sunshine Wall because protection pulled out.)

FALL ON ROCK, INADEQUATE PROTECTION
West Virginia, Nelson Rocks Preserve

West Virginia State Police say Amanda Joy Crawford was climbing a "via ferrata" (iron way) at the Nelson Rocks Preserve in Pendleton County when she unhooked one of her lines to go around a tree, mis-stepped, and fell almost 150 feet. She was pronounced dead at the scene.

The type of mountain climbing Crawford was doing is rare in the United States. It's a system that is said to be safe for people who have no prior climbing training. We spoke with an Eastern Mennonite University professor who is familiar with via ferratas. He says this type of climbing is designed to prevent any accidents. The route Crawford was climbing was only the second of its kind in the United States. (Source: From an article by Lauren McKay)

(Editor's Note: There may be more than two via ferratas in the U.S. There is one such route on Half Dome in Yosemite National Park that has been climbed by

thousands without incident. A few individuals have attempted to establish more via ferratas in the U.S., but most are opposed to this because of the level of destruction it causes to the rock. There are a lot of websites to go to, including www.nelsonrocks. org, to learn about these. Also go to Google and just put in via ferrata.)

FALL ON SNOW—SKI MOUNTAINEERING
Wyoming, Grand Tetons

On March 2, while ski-mountaineering, Ben Morley (23) was descending an area near the Southwest Couloir of the Middle Teton on skis. He hit a patch of ice on his skis, lost control, and fell 500 feet where he impacted a rocky area and stopped. Morley sustained injuries to his hip and leg.

At the time of the incident, Grand Teton National Park did not have a local helicopter resource on contract. The Teton County SAR helicopter was contacted and secured on an Aircraft Rental Agreement (ARA). Based on the initial report from Wright, the condition of the patient, and area resources, Rangers Jackson and Torres would initiate a response. They would fly to the area by helicopter, locate, evaluate, package, and lower the patient to an area where he would be transferred to the helicopter and flown to St. John's Hospital. Because of high winds, darkness, and deteriorating weather conditions, Jackson and Torres would need to spend the night with Morley. The plan also involved sending rangers up Garnet Canyon with support equipment to the rescue scene.

Jackson and Torres arrived on scene at 2205. They began to evaluate and treat the patient. McConnell arrived on scene at 0230. Guerrieri and Byerly arrived at 0415. At first light, Jackson was able to evaluate the weather conditions near the scene. He advised me that the wind was too high to safely land the helicopter nearby. Morley was lowered approximately 1000 feet to an area near the Ellingwood Couloir. Helicopter 9MA landed and Morley was loaded inside, attended by Torres, and transported to the hanger at 0954. Morley was transported from the helicopter to Medic 1, then taken to St. John's Hospital.

Analysis

I interviewed the victim, Ben Morley, at his hospital room at 1430. Morley stated that he, Patrick Wright, and Josh Schear had left Taggart Lake parking lot between 10:00 and 10:30 a.m. on March 2. They had planned on climbing, then skiing the Southwest Couloir of the Middle Teton. About 200-300 feet from the summit, they encountered too much rock to ski, so they left their skis in the couloir and finished the climb. After reaching the summit, they returned to their skis and began their ski descent. They made it out the couloir and began to descend into the South Fork of Garnet Canyon. Shortly after 5:00 p.m., Wright and Schear stopped below Morley.

As Morely started to ski down the snowfield, he encountered a patch of ice. His skis lost their edging and came off, causing him to fall and begin to slide out of control. Wright started to move into Morley's path, thinking that he could maybe slow him down, but decided that Morley was moving too fast and abandoned the idea. Morley slid approximately 500 feet before hitting a rocky area where he came to rest. Morley had an ice ax in his pack, but he did not have self-arrest ski poles and was not wearing a helmet. Morley stated that he had grown up skiing, having skied since he was about two or three years old.

Morely is a young and fit individual and a very competent skier. Morley had an event occur to him that happens to all skiers sometime in their careers. Unfortunately, this did not happen at a ski area but instead occurred in the backcountry. Morley slid a long distance, hitting a rocky area. The impact with rocks caused his injury. It also saved him from sliding several hundred more feet and sustaining more serious injuries or death. The snow conditions they were skiing were considered to be fairly soft, so to ski with an ice ax may have been overly cumbersome. Though it is difficult to speculate, self-arrest ski poles that are made for ski-mountaineering may have had good results.

This rescue involved using specialized personnel who are competent at ascending and descending steep ice and snow on skis. The personnel and specialized equipment used for this rescue were exposed to a variety of hazardous terrain and weather conditions during the operation. Remarkably, there were no injuries sustained during the operation. (Source: Edited from a report by Chris Harder, Ranger and Incident Commander)

FALL ON ROCK
Wyoming, Grand Teton National Park, Garnet Canyon

On July 22 at 1445, Teton Dispatch forwarded a cellphone caller to me. John Coombs who told me that Eva Bell (22) a member of his party, had fallen and tumbled approximately 80 to 100 feet at the base of the Open Book route in Garnet Canyon. He told me that she fell on very steep ground for about 20 feet and then tumbled and cartwheeled another 60 to 80 feet on lower angle rocky terrain. He told me that she did not lose consciousness and that she was alert and oriented. He said that she had lower lumbar pain, left rib pain, an impact injury to her face and multiple abrasions and lacerations. He also said that there was a wilderness first responder on scene. Coombs had had to hike about 1.5 miles down canyon to make the cell call. I told him to return to the accident site where he could stay until help arrived, unless Bell's condition had worsened. If that were the case, he was to call me again. I had Ranger Visnovske, (park medic) take an additional medical report from Coombs. Visnovske then contacted medical director Will Smith with the patient information.

Via Park Dispatch, the contract helicopter was requested. They gave an ETA of over one hour. Available rescue personnel were summoned to the rescue cache. Rangers Byerly and Hardesty were sent to the scene by foot given the long helicopter response time. They arrived about the same time that contract helicopter 20HX arrived at Lupine Meadows. Hardesty and Byerly assessed Bell's injuries and determined that the best method for extraction would be to use the patient evacuation suit. After a mission briefing, Rangers Jackson, Visnovske, and Motter were flown to a staging site at the Garnet Meadows. Jackson spotted as the evacuation suit was delivered via short-haul to the accident site. Bell was then extracted unattended and flown to the Garnet Meadows landing zone where she was loaded internally in the helicopter and flown to Lupine Meadows. She was transported to St. John's Hospital in Medic 1. All rescue personnel were flown back to Lupine Meadows from the Garnet Canyon Meadows.

Analysis

In an interview at St. John's Hospital, Bell and her companions told me that they were soloing the 4th class terrain just below the Open Book climb. Bell's friends told me that she became uncomfortable with the climbing and was about to pass her backpack up to a companion when she slipped and fell. She was not yet wearing a climbing helmet or climbing shoes. Coombs told me that he felt the fact that Bell had her pack on when she fell saved her from further trauma. (Source: Scott Guenther, Ranger and Incident Commander)

HAND-HOLDS BROKE OFF—FALL ON ROCK
Wyoming, Grand Teton National Park, Direct Jensen Ridge

On August 5 about 1430, Exum Guide Mark Newcomb (39) fell about 80 feet when his hand-holds broke off while ascending the Direct Jensen Ridge route of Symmetry Spire. He was about two pitches from the top of the technical portion of the route. He was guiding two clients, and one of them was belaying him, arresting his fall despite suffering a significant wound to his right forearm from a falling rock. Newcomb suffered multiple trauma, including lacerations, bruises, and abrasions. The Exum Mountaineering Guides office was immediately notified of the accident via cellphone.

Rescue Coordinator G. Montopoli was contacted by the Exum Mountaineering Guides office, and after speaking with a client and Newcomb, immediately initiated a rescue operation. The contract helicopter was summoned to Lupine Meadows and St. John's Hospital Emergency Room was advised of the situation.

Rangers D. Bywater and E. Visnovske were climbing in the area (Baxter's Pinnacle) and were dispatched to the scene on foot in the event that an approaching thunderstorm precluded use of the helicopter.

At 1530, an initial reconnaissance flight was conducted to determine the technical requirements for the rescue operation. Two rangers, A. Byerly and H. Motter, were then inserted on the first flight. On the second flight, two more rangers, R. Jackson and J. McConnell, were inserted. The helicopter flew around the scene while the two clients were loaded into evacuation suits and were then extracted from the scene to Lupine Meadows.

A rescue litter was then delivered at about 1630 hours to the accident scene. After medically assessing and treating Newcomb, he was immobilized on a backboard and placed in the litter. The litter was extracted from the scene and delivered to Lupine Meadows via short-haul techniques at 1715. Newcomb was then transported to St. John's Hospital, Jackson, WY, via GTNP ambulance.

After a thorough medical evaluation at the hospital, M. Newcomb was released that evening after treatment for his injuries. (Source: George Montopoli, Ranger and Incident Commander)

FALL ON ROCK, CLIMBING ALONE AND UNROPED
Wyoming, Wind River Range, Mount Bonneville

On September 6, Ken Koski (56) fell to his death while either ascending or descending the Southeast Ridge of Mount Bonneville. He was in 4th and 5th class terrain.

An extensive and expensive search eventually discovered his body 4-500 feet below the ridge. His journal was a huge asset in this search. It described him slipping twice in 3rd class terrain in two days, which helped searchers focus their efforts on the area beneath the exposed ridge.

Analysis

Ken was climbing alone and unroped. None of the local guides knew of an unroped route up Mount Bonneville. But Ken's journal mentioned a chimney he saw in a guide book that none of us are familiar with. This chimney is supposed to be key to sneaking up Mount Bonneville, and Ken's journal indicated that he had found the chimney during his aborted attempt on September 4. Based on routine journal entries that ended on September 5, we believe he died on the 6th, on his 56th birthday. (Source: John Gookin, SAR Commander, Fremont County Sheriff's Office)

(Editor's Note: There were no reports of accidents from any other Wyoming climbing sites.)

STATISTICAL TABLES

TABLE I
REPORTED MOUNTAINEERING ACCIDENTS

	Number of Accidents Reported		Total Persons Involved		Injured		Fatalities	
	USA	CAN	USA	CAN	USA	CAN	USA	CAN
1951	15		22		11		3	
1952	31		35		17		13	
1953	24		27		12		12	
1954	31		41		31		8	
1955	34		39		28		6	
1956	46		72		54		13	
1957	45		53		28		18	
1958	32		39		23		11	
1959	42	2	56	2	31	0	19	2
1960	47	4	64	12	37	8	19	4
1961	49	9	61	14	45	10	14	4
1962	71	1	90	1	64	0	19	1
1963	68	11	79	12	47	10	19	2
1964	53	11	65	16	44	10	14	3
1965	72	0	90	0	59	0	21	0
1966	67	7	80	9	52	6	16	3
1967	74	10	110	14	63	7	33	5
1968	70	13	87	19	43	12	27	5
1969	94	11	125	17	66	9	29	2
1970	129	11	174	11	88	5	15	5
1971	110	17	138	29	76	11	31	7
1972	141	29	184	42	98	17	49	13
1973	108	6	131	6	85	4	36	2
1974	96	7	177	50	75	1	26	5
1975	78	7	158	22	66	8	19	2
1976	137	16	303	31	210	9	53	6
1977	121	30	277	49	106	21	32	11
1978	118	17	221	19	85	6	42	10
1979	100	36	137	54	83	17	40	19
1980	191	29	295	85	124	26	33	8
1981	97	43	223	119	80	39	39	6
1982	140	48	305	126	120	43	24	14
1983	187	29	442	76	169	26	37	7
1984	182	26	459	63	174	15	26	6
1985	195	27	403	62	190	22	17	3
1986	203	31	406	80	182	25	37	14

	Number of Accidents Reported		Total Persons Involved		Injured		Fatalities	
	USA	**CAN**	**USA**	**CAN**	**USA**	**CAN**	**USA**	**CAN**
1987	192	25	377	79	140	23	32	9
1988	156	18	288	44	155	18	24	4
1989	141	18	272	36	124	11	17	9
1990	136	25	245	50	125	24	24	4
1991	169	20	302	66	147	11	18	6
1992	175	17	351	45	144	11	43	6
1993	132	27	274	50	121	17	21	1
1994	158	25	335	58	131	25	27	5
1995	168	24	353	50	134	18	37	7
1996	139	28	261	59	100	16	31	6
1997	158	35	323	87	148	24	31	13
1998	138	24	281	55	138	18	20	1
1999	123	29	248	69	91	20	17	10
2000	150	23	301	36	121	23	24	7
2001	150	22	276	47	138	14	16	2
2002	139	27	295	29	105	23	34	6
2003	118	29	231	32	105	22	18	6
2004	160	35	311	30	140	16	35	14
2005	111	19	176	41	85	14	34	7
2006	109		227		89		21	
TOTALS	**6,220**	**958**	**11,325**	**2003**	**5,247**	**715**	**1,394**	**292**

TABLE II

Geographical Districts	1951–2005 Number of Accidents	Deaths	Total Persons Involved	2006 Number of Accidents	Deaths	Total Persons Involved
CANADA						
Alberta	520	142	1033			
British Columbia	317	119	641			
Yukon Territory	37	28	77			
New Brunswick	1	0	0			
Ontario	37	9	67			
Quebec	31	10	63			
East Arctic	8	2	21			
West Arctic	2	2	2			
Practice Cliffs[1]	20	2	36			
UNITED STATES						
Alaska	480	178	803	19	5	41
Arizona, Nevada Texas	87	18	153	3	0	7
Atlantic–North	933	146	1599	23	1	47
Atlantic–South	96	24	166	2	1	3
California	1243	290	2478	22	4	39
Central	133	16	215	1	1	2
Colorado	740	208	2255	15	4	33
Montana, Idaho South Dakota	78	31	124	1	1	2
Oregon	195	107	440	5	3	14
Utah, New Mexico	159	58	289	3	0	10
Washington	1028	317	851	8	0	16
Wyoming	546	127	984	7	1	13

[1]This category includes bouldering, artificial climbing walls, buildings, and so forth. These are also added to the count of each province, but not to the total count, though that error has been made in previous years. The Practice Cliffs category has been removed from the U.S. data.

TABLE III

	1951–05 USA	1959–05 CAN.	2006 USA	2006 CAN.
Terrain				
Rock	4310	528	68	
Snow	2268	355	36	
Ice	254	158	5	
River	14	3	0	
Unknown	22	10	0	
Ascent or Descent				
Ascent	2853	587	73	
Descent	2192	371	35	
Unknown	248	13	1	
Other[N.B.]	7	0	0	
Immediate Cause				
Fall or slip on rock	3407	290	60	
Slip on snow or ice	971	207	19	
Falling rock, ice, or object	610	137	4	
Exceeding abilities	535	32	5	
Illness[1]	375	26	7	
Stranded	329	53	6	
Avalanche	284	127	2	
Exposure	265	14	5	
Rappel Failure/Error[2]	274	47	10	
Loss of control/glissade	199	17	7	
Nut/chock pulled out	196	9	10	
Failure to follow route	176	30	3	
Fall into crevasse/moat	153	50	6	
Piton/ice screw pulled out	95	13	0	
Faulty use of crampons	95	6	7	
Lightning	46	7	0	
Skiing[3]	53	11	2	
Ascending too fast	65	0	0	
Equipment failure	14	3	1	
Other[4]	413	37	25	
Unknown	61	10	0	
Contributory Causes				
Climbing unroped	987	165	17	
Exceeding abilities	885	202	10	
Placed no/inadequate protection			15	
Inadequate equipment/clothing	664	70	8	
Weather	462	67	5	
Climbing alone	389	69	5	
No hard hat	327	71	10	

	1951–05 USA	1959–05 CAN	2006 USA	2006 CAN
Contributory Causes (continued)				
Nut/chock pulled out	199	32	0	
Inadequate belay	197	28	5	
Poor position	166	20	2	
Darkness	140	21	1	
Party separated	115	12	2	
Failure to test holds	97	32	3	
Piton/ice screw pulled out	86	13	0	
Failed to follow directions	73	12	0	
Exposure	59	16	5	
Illness[1]	40	9	0	
Equipment failure	11	7	0	
Other[4]	256	100	4	
Age of Individuals				
Under 15	1243	12	0	
15-20	1258	203	8	
21-25	1358	257	30	
26-30	1257	211	16	
31-35	1051	114	12	
36-50	1177	143	30	
Over 50	217	31	9	
Unknown	1947	530	22	
Experience Level				
None/Little	1739	304	20	
Moderate (1 to 3 years)	1575	354	20	
Experienced	1855	440	47	
Unknown	1983	559	42	
Month of Year				
January	218	25	6	
February	202	55	4	
March	299	68	4	
April	397	39	4	
May	882	62	18	
June	1026	70	18	
July	1109	254	12	
August	1011	184	16	
September	1155	75	10	
October	439	42	9	
November	184	20	4	
December	93	24	4	
Unknown	17	1	0	
Type of Injury/Illness (Data since 1984)				
Fracture	1171	223	48	
Laceration	670	71	15	

	1951–05 USA	1959–05 CAN	2006 USA	2006 CAN
Type of Injury/Illness (Data since 1984) (continued)				
Abrasion	321	76	9	
Bruise	450	83	12	
Sprain/strain	314	33	17	
Concussion	215	28	10	
Hypothermia	152	16	2	
Frostbite	120	12	5	
Dislocation	113	16	4	
Puncture	43	13	1	
Acute Mountain Sickness	42	0	1	
HAPE	68	0	3	
HACE	24	0	1	
Other[5]	302	49	13	
None	224	188	14	

N.B. Some accidents happen when climbers are at the top or bottom of a route, not climbing. They may be setting up a belay or rappel or are just not anchored when they fall. (This category created in 2001. The category unknown is primarily because of solo climbers.)

[1]These illnesses/injuries, which led directly or indirectly to the accident, include: severe ischemia & coronary occlusion, HAPE, HACE, AMS, frostbite, pneumonia, corneal abrasion, burns (2), panic attack, mental breakdown, hypothermia, myocardial infarction, and fatigue (4).

[2]These include inadequate anchors, rappelled off the end of the rope, uneven ropes, harness loop broke, inattention by belayers when lowering.

[3]This category was set up originally for ski mountaineering. Backcountry touring or snowshoeing incidents—even if one gets avalanched—are not in the data.

[4]These include: unable to self-arrest (5), lowering errors (5), late start (3) hand- or foot-hold broke off (5), rope-drag, disappeared, fuel bottle blew up, rope stuck in crack, via ferrata, weighted leg incorrectly—so dislocated knee, climbing rope under leg while leading—so climber turned upside down in fall, jumped off boulder, client falls into another client on fixed rope (Denali), failed to follow avalanche advisory.

[5]These include: severe ischemia & coronary occlusion, pneumonia, corneal abrasion, burns —fuel bottle explosion (2) and rope (2), panic attack, mental breakdown, hypothermia, myocardial infarction, and fatigue

(Editor's Note: Under the category "other," many of the particular items will have been recorded under a general category. For example, the climber who dislodges a rock that falls on another climber would be coded as Falling Rock/Object. A climber who has a hand- or foot-hold come loose and falls would be coded as Fall On Rock and Other—and most often includes Failure To Test Holds.)

MOUNTAIN RESCUE UNITS IN NORTH AMERICA
**Denotes team fully certified—Technical Rock,
Snow & Ice, Wilderness Search;
S, R, SI = certified partially in Search, Rock, and/or Snow & Ice

ALASKA
Alaska Mountain Rescue Group. PO Box 241102, Anchorage,
AK 99524. www.amrg.org

Denali National Park SAR. PO Box 588, Talkeetna, AK 99676.
Dena_talkeetna@nps.gov

US Army Alaskan Warfare Training Center. #2900 501 Second St., APO AP 96508

ARIZONA
Apache Rescue Team. PO Box 100, St. Johns, AZ 85936

Arizona Department Of Public Safety Air Rescue. Phoenix, Flagstaff, Tucson,
Kingman, AZ

Arizona Division Of Emergency Services. Phoenix, AZ

Grand Canyon National Park Rescue Team. PO Box 129, Grand Canyon, AZ 86023

**Central Arizona Mountain Rescue Team/Maricopa County Sheriff's Office
MR.** PO Box 4004 Phoenix, AZ 85030. www.mcsomr.org

Sedona Fire District Special Operations Rescue Team. 2860 Southwest Dr.,
Sedona, AZ 86336. ropes@sedona.net

Southern Arizona Rescue Assn/Pima County Sheriff's Office. PO Box 12892,
Tucson, AZ 85732. http://hambox.theriver.com/sarci/sara01.html

CALIFORNIA
Altadena Mountain Rescue Team. 780 E. Altadena Dr., Altadena, CA 91001
www.altadenasheriffs.org/rescue/amrt.html

Bay Area Mountain Rescue Team. PO Box 19184, Stanford, CA 94309 bamru@
hooked.net

California Office of Emergency Services. 2800 Meadowview Rd., Sacramento, CA.
95832. warning.center@oes.ca.gov

China Lake Mountain Rescue Group. PO Box 2037, Ridgecrest, CA 93556
www.clmrg.org

Inyo County Sheriff's Posse SAR. PO Box 982, Bishop, CA 93514 inyocosar@
juno.com

Joshua Tree National Park SAR. 74485 National Monument Drive,
Twenty Nine Palms, CA 92277. patrick_suddath@nps.gov

Los Padres SAR Team. PO Box 6602, Santa Barbara, CA 93160-6602

Malibu Mountain Rescue Team. PO Box 222, Malibu, CA 90265.
www.mmrt.org

Montrose SAR Team. PO Box 404, Montrose, CA 91021

Riverside Mountain Rescue Unit. PO Box 5444, Riverside,
CA 92517. www.rmru.org   rmru@bigfoot.com

San Bernardino County Sheriff's Cave Rescue Team. 655 E. Third St.
San Bernardino, CA 92415
www.sbsd-vfu.org/units/SAR/SAR203/sar203_1.htm

San Bernardino County So/ West Valley SAR. 13843 Peyton Dr., Chino Hills, CA
91709.

San Diego Mountain Rescue Team. PO Box 81602, San Diego, CA 92138. www.sdmrt.org

San Dimas Mountain Rescue Team. PO Box 35, San Dimas, CA 91773

Santa Clarita Valley SAR / L.A.S.O. 23740 Magic Mountain Parkway, Valencia, CA 91355. http://members.tripod.com/scvrescue/

Sequoia-Kings Canyon National Park Rescue Team. Three Rivers, CA 93271

Sierra Madre SAR. PO Box 24, Sierra Madre, CA 91025. www.mra.org/smsrt.html

Ventura County SAR. 2101 E. Olson Rd, Thousand Oaks, CA 91362 www.vcsar.org

Yosemite National Park Rescue Team. PO Box 577-SAR, Yosemite National Park, CA 95389

COLORADO

Alpine Rescue Team. PO Box 934, Evergreen, CO 80439 www.heart-beat-of-evergreen.com/alpine/alpine.html

Colorado Ground SAR. 2391 Ash St, Denver, CO 80222 www.coloradowingcap.org/CGSART/Default.htm

Crested Butte SAR. PO Box 485, Crested Butte, CO 81224

Douglas County Search And Rescue. PO Box 1102, Castle Rock, CO 80104. www.dcsarco.org info@dcsarco.org

El Paso County SAR. 3950 Interpark Dr, Colorado Springs, CO 80907-9028. www.epcsar.org

Eldorado Canyon State Park. PO Box B, Eldorado Springs, CO 80025

Grand County SAR. Box 172, Winter Park, CO 80482

Larimer County SAR. 1303 N. Shields St., Fort Collins, CO 80524. www.fortnet. org/LCSAR/ lcsar@co.larimer.co.us

Mountain Rescue Aspen. 630 W. Main St, Aspen, CO 81611 www.mountainrescueaspen.org

Park County SAR, CO. PO Box 721, Fairplay, CO 80440

Rocky Mountain National Park Rescue Team. Estes Park, CO 80517

Rocky Mountain Rescue Group. PO Box Y, Boulder, CO 80306 www.colorado.edu/StudentGroups/rmrg/ rmrg@colorado.edu

Routt County SAR. PO Box 772837, Steamboat Springs, CO 80477 RCSAR@co.routt.co.us

Summit County Rescue Group. PO Box 1794, Breckenridge, CO 80424

Vail Mountain Rescue Group. PO Box 1597, Vail, CO 81658 http://sites.netscape.net/vailmra/homepage vmrg@vail.net

Western State College Mountain Rescue Team. Western State College Union, Gunnison, CO 81231. org_mrt@western.edu

IDAHO

Bonneville County SAR. 605 N. Capital Ave, Idaho Falls, ID 83402 www.srv.net/~jrcase/bcsar.html

Idaho Mountain SAR. PO Box 741, Boise, ID 83701. www.imsaru.org rsksearch@aol.com

MAINE

Acadia National Park SAR. Bar Harbor, Maine

MARYLAND
Maryland Sar Group. 5434 Vantage Point Road, Columbia, MD 21044
Peter_McCabe@Ed.gov

MONTANA
Glacier National Park SAR. PO Box 128, Glacier National Park,
West Glacier, MT 59936
Flathead County Search and Rescue. 920 South Main St., Kalispell, MT 59901.
Sheriff's Office phone: 406-758-5585.

NEVADA
Las Vegas Metro PD SAR. 4810 Las Vegas Blvd., South Las Vegas,
NV 89119. www.lvmpdsar.com

NEW MEXICO
Albuquerque Mountain Rescue Council. PO Box 53396, Albuquerque,
NM 87153. www.abq.com/amrc/ albrescu@swcp.com

NEW HAMPSHIRE
Appalachian Mountain Club. Pinkham Notch Camp, Gorham, NH 03581
Mountain Rescue Service. PO Box 494, North Conway, NH 03860

NEW YORK
76 SAR. 243 Old Quarry Rd., Feura Bush, NY 12067
Mohonk Preserve Rangers. PO Box 715, New Paltz, NY 12561
NY State Forest Rangers. 50 Wolf Rd., Room 440C, Albany, NY 12233

OREGON
Corvallis Mountain Rescue Unit. PO Box 116, Corvallis, OR 97339
www.cmrv.peak.org
Deschutes County SAR. 63333 West Highway 20, Bend, OR 97701
Eugene Mountain Rescue. PO Box 20, Eugene, OR 97440
Hood River Crag Rats Rescue Team. 2880 Thomsen Rd., Hood River,
OR 97031
Portland Mountain Rescue. PO Box 5391, Portland, OR 97228
www.pmru.org info@pmru.org

PENNSYLVANNIA
Allegheny Mountain Rescue Group. c/o Mercy Hospital,
1400 Locust, Pittsburgh, PA 15219. www.asrc.net/amrg
Wilderness Emergency Strike Team. 11 North Duke Street, Lancaster,
PA 17602. www.west610.org

UTAH
Davis County Sheriff's SAR. PO Box 800, Farmington, UT 84025
www.dcsar.org
Rocky Mountain Rescue Dogs. 3353 S. Main #122, Salt Lake City, UT 84115
Salt Lake County Sheriff's SAR. 3510 South 700 West, Salt Lake City, UT 84119
San Juan County Emergency Services. PO Box 9, Monticello, UT 84539

**Utah County Sherrif's SAR. PO Box 330, Provo, UT 84603. ucsar@utah.uswest.net

**Weber County Sheriff's Mountain Rescue. 745 Nancy Dr, Ogden, UT 84403. http://planet.weber.edu/mru

Zion National Park SAR. Springdale, UT 84767

VERMONT
**Stowe Hazardous Terrain Evacuation. P.O. Box 291, Stowe, VT 05672 www.stowevt.org/htt/

VIRGINIA
Air Force Rescue Coordination Center. Suite 101, 205 Dodd Building, Langley AFB, VA 23665. www2.acc.af.mil/afrcc/airforce.rescue@usa.net

WASHINGTON STATE
**Bellingham Mountain Rescue Council. PO Box 292, Bellingham, WA 98225

**Central Washington Mountain Rescue Council. PO Box 2663, Yakima, WA 98907. www.nwinfo.net/~cwmr/ cwmr@nwinfo.net

**Everett Mountain Rescue Unit, Inc. 5506 Old Machias Road, Snohomish, WA 98290-5574. emrui@aol.com

Mount Rainier National Park Rescue Team. Longmire, WA 98397

North Cascades National Park Rescue Team. 728 Ranger Station Rd, Marblemount, WA 98267

**Olympic Mountain Rescue. PO Box 4244, Bremerton, WA 98312 www.olympicmountainrescue.org information@olympicmountainrescue.org

Olympic National Park Rescue Team. 600 Park Ave, Port Angeles, WA 98362

**Seattle Mountain Rescue. PO Box 67, Seattle, WA 98111 www.eskimo.com/~pc22/SMR/smr.html

**Skagit Mountain Rescue. PO Box 2, Mt. Vernon, WA 98273

**Tacoma Mountain Rescue. PO Box 696, Tacoma, WA 98401 www.tmru.org

North Country Volcano Rescue Team. 404 S. Parcel Ave, Yacolt, WA 98675 www.northcountryems.org/vrt/index.html

WASHINGTON, DC
National Park Service, EMS/SAR Division. Washington, DC

US Park Police Aviation. Washington, DC

WYOMING
Grand Teton National Park Rescue Team. PO Box 67, Moose, WY 83012

Park County SAR, WY. Park County SO, 1131 11th, Cody, WY 82412

CANADA
North Shore Rescue Team. 147 E. 14th St, North Vancouver, B.C., Canada V7L 2N4

**Rocky Mountain House SAR. Box 1888, Rocky Mountain House, Alberta, Canada T0M 1T0

MOUNTAIN RESCUE ASSOCIATION

PO Box 880868
San Diego, CA 92168-0868
www.mra.org • www.mountainrescuehonorguard.org

Fran Sharp, President
Tacoma Mountain Rescue Unit, WA
thegirlpilot@hotmail.com
253-691-3773 (phone)   360-482-6187 (fax)
Term expires June 2008

Charley Shimanski, Vice President
Alpine Rescue Team, CO
shimanski@speedtrail.net
303-674-7937 (home)   303-909-9348 (cell)
303-201-2900 (pager)
Term expires June 2008

Dan Land, Secretary/Treasurer/CFO
San Dimas Mountain Rescue Team
wdland13@yahoo.com
909-268-2237 (cell)   909-621-9988 (home)
Term expires June 2007

Glenn Henderson, Member at Large
Riverside Mountain Rescue, CA
glennrobin@hotmail.com
951-925-4848 (home)   951-317-5635 (cell)
Term expires 2008

Neil Van Dyke, Member at Large
Stowe Hazardous Terrain Evacuation Team, VT
neilvd@stoweagle.com
802-253-8003 (work)
Term expires June 2007

Kayley Trujillo, Executive Secretary/Treasurer
978 Camino de la Reina #34
San Diego, CA 92108
kayley@kayley.com
858-229-4295 (phone)   619-374-7072 (fax)
(Appointed position)